D1060066

Queen Elizabeth II

Commemorating the Diamond Jubilee

Queen Elizabeth II
Commemorating the Diamond Jubilee

Times Books
An imprint of HarperCollins Publishers
Westerhill Road, Bishopbriggs, Glasgow G64 2QT

First Published 2012

Text written by Christopher Riches and Richard Happer

Printed in the United Kingdom by Butler Tanner and Dennis Ltd, Frome

British Library Cataloguing in Publication Data
A catalogue record for this book is available from the British Library

ISBN 978 0 00 792481 3

Imp 001

If you would like to comment on any aspect of this book, please write to:
Times Atlases, HarperCollins Publishers, Westerhill Road, Bishopbriggs, Glasgow G64 2QT
e-mail: timesatlas@harpercollins.co.uk
or visit our website at: www.timesatlas.com
twitter.com/timesatlas

THE TIMES

Queen Elizabeth II

Commemorating the Diamond Jubilee

Contents

The Early Years

Princess Elizabeth at her desk in her sitting room at Buckingham Palace, 19 September 1946.

The Early Years

The year 2012 is the Diamond Jubilee of Queen Elizabeth II, the second-longest reigning monarch after Queen Victoria, and it is in the twilight years of Victoria's reign that our story begins, with the birth of Elizabeth's father in 1895, two years before Victoria celebrated her own Diamond Jubilee. Prince Albert Frederick Arthur George was the second son of Prince George, Duke of York, and so a great-grandson of Queen Victoria. He was named Albert as the day of his birth (14 December) was the anniversary of the death of Victoria's beloved consort Albert, who died in 1861.

As a second son, Bertie, as he was known in the family, was not considered likely to become monarch and he grew up as a shy man whose health was not robust. He trained as a naval officer, and was afflicted by a stammer that was to blight his moments of public speaking, a story now well-known through the sympathetic film, *The King's Speech*. On Queen Victoria's death in 1901, his

^
Queen Victoria at Osborne House on the Isle of Wight with some of her great-grandchildren, the children of the Duke and Duchess of York. Victoria is holding Prince Henry, Princess Mary is on the chair, Prince Albert ('Bertie') sitting in the foreground and Prince Edward is standing.

grandfather became King Edward VII and, after Edward's death in 1910, his father became King George V while his mother, Mary of Teck, became Queen Mary. Bertie served in the Royal Navy during World War I, taking part in the indecisive Battle of Jutland in 1916, and at the end of the war, gained a pilot's licence in the newly-formed Royal Air Force. In 1920 he was created Duke of York and started undertaking Royal functions. While his outgoing elder brother Edward toured the world with enthusiasm, Bertie visited factories, gaining the nickname of 'the Industrial Prince'. Bertie wished for a quiet and stable life which he hoped to share with Elizabeth Bowes-Lyon, daughter of the Earl and Countess of Strathmore and Kinghorne. Elizabeth, born on 4 August 1900, was lively and outgoing and attracted the attention of Bertie, who made a number of proposals of marriage to her over a two-year period, finally winning her acceptance in January 1923. They were married at Westminster Abbey on 26 April 1923, amidst great celebrations.

^
The wedding of Prince Albert with Elizabeth Bowes-Lyon in 1923. Prince Albert's parents are on the right and Elizabeth's on the left.

The birth of Elizabeth

Three years later, on 21 April 1926, their first child was born at the Strathmore's London house, 17 Bruton Street in Mayfair, and she was named Elizabeth (after her mother) Alexandra (after her great-grandmother and consort of Edward VII, who had died the previous year) Mary (after her grandmother Queen Mary, wife of George V). Just over a month later, on 29 May, after the disruptions of the General Strike were over, she made her first public appearance, travelling from Bruton Street to Buckingham Palace for her christening, wearing the christening robe first worn in 1840 by Victoria, Queen Victoria's first daughter.

Under the care of the Duchess of York's former nanny Clara ('Alla') Knight, described as 'unmodern to a fault', patterns in the princess's life soon emerged – summer visits to Glamis Castle, Christmas at Sandringham and adjusting to absent parents, for in January 1927 Bertie and Elizabeth set sail for Australia via Panama, Fiji and New Zealand, to open the Federal Parliament Building in the very new capital city of Canberra, founded in 1913. One of the stars of the trip, however, was happily playing back home, for Princess Elizabeth (she was called Betty by the Australian press) was the centre of much fascination to those who flocked to see her parents – indeed it was estimated that she was given three tons of toys as presents. Her parents returned in late June having missed nearly six months of Elizabeth's life – by all accounts it took a little while for Elizabeth to sort out who 'Mummy' really was.

^
The Duchess of York with Princess Elizabeth in 1926.

Pictures of Princess Elizabeth's childhood. >

Growing up

In late 1927 the family moved into their own townhouse in London at 145 Piccadilly, across Green Park from Buckingham Palace. Elizabeth occupied a day and night nursery on the top floor overlooking the park and was ruled over by Alla, who instilled a regime of order, tidiness, manners and acceptance, enforcing such rules as playing with only one toy at a time. In 1928 the Duke and Duchess hired Nasby Hall in Northamptonshire for the hunting season and so began Elizabeth's delight in horses and dogs, an enthusiasm which has stayed with her ever since. It was around this time that she built a close relationship with her somewhat forbidding grandfather, charming him in a way that his own sons were clearly unable to do, and she certainly played a part in assisting his recuperation at Bognor from a bout of illness in 1929 – indeed the *Daily Mail* reported that she would sit with him and make 'the most amusing and original comments on people and events', though she would be sure not to forget to curtsey when leaving the room, as was only right to do.

Lilibet, as her family nickname became (based around her early attempts to say her own name), then had to adjust to the arrival of a sibling, for on 21 August 1930, at Glamis Castle, Margaret Rose was born. The family, 'Us Four' as described by the Duke of York, settled into new domestic ways. From 1931 the Royal Lodge in Windsor Great Park became their country retreat at a time when the Duke did not have an onerous round of public duties. He spent much time with his two daughters, who could also delight in the splendid gift of a miniature Welsh Cottage, Y Bwythyn Bach ('The Little House'), a two-thirds size, fully-equipped thatched cottage entirely made in Wales, that was presented to Elizabeth on her sixth birthday. It was a dream present for any child, containing all that should be in a house, from electric lighting to miniature books and a radio and plumbing that worked. The cottage is still in the grounds of the Royal Lodge, and was recently refurbished by Princess Beatrice.

The princesses were educated privately, with much of the teaching in the hands of Marion Crawford ('Crawfie'), who arrived in 1933, aged twenty-two, as a recent graduate from Moray House Training College in Edinburgh. She stayed with the princesses until 1947. Theirs was an education designed to inculcate good manners and an enquiring mind. Crawfie was aware how insulated from the real world the princesses were, and while recognizing that this was inevitable, did bring some normality to their lives, from the establishment of a Buckingham Palace Girl Guides troop to taking the princesses on a trip on the London Underground. Queen Mary was particularly interested in the princesses' education, suggesting appropriate reading and 'instructive entertainments' such as a trip to the Tower of London. In 1947 Crawfie resigned in order to marry, a little ahead of Elizabeth's wedding, and under some marital pressure decided to sell her story in a book called *The Little Princesses*. Though the book was sympathetic, it broke a cardinal rule of Royal

^
The Princesses visit London Zoo in 1938 under the watchful eye of Crawfie (in the centre).

employment, that no details of Royal life should be reported. Its publication rapidly ended any Royal connections she had and left us with the phrase 'doing a Crawfie' for anyone selling family secrets for personal gain. There were some more formal strands to Elizabeth's education as the years advanced, most notably from the Vice Provost of Eton College, Sir Henry Marten, who provided instruction on the British Constitution, and from Vicomte de Bellaigue, who taught French, French literature and European history.

In 1935, there were great celebrations for the Silver Jubilee of George V and 'Us Four' rode in a carriage to a service of celebration in St Paul's Cathedral. However, George V was in poor health and on 15 January of the following year, while staying at Sandringham he took to his bed and gradually grew weaker and died on the evening of 21 January. While George V had not courted public attention, he had become a father figure of the country and nearly one million people paid tribute to him as he lay in state in Westminster Hall, the new monarch and his three brothers at one point providing the guard of honour around his coffin. He was buried at Windsor.

^
Princesses Elizabeth and Margaret waving from the balcony at Buckingham Palace during the celebrations of the Silver Jubilee of King George V. The King looks indulgently at Elizabeth, who softened his stiff character.

The Abdication crisis

The Prince of Wales became king, as Edward VIII, with Elizabeth becoming second in line to the throne, after her father. However, events in late 1936 transformed the lives of 'Us Four'. Until 2 December the British public and most people in authority had been unaware that the King wished to marry Wallis Simpson, an American divorcee. Edward first met Wallis Simpson in 1931, had holidayed with her and brought her to Buckingham Palace in 1934. Matters took a more serious turn once he became king. In August 1936 he, Mrs Simpson and some friends went on a cruise in the Adriatic and photographs appeared in European newspapers. Behind the scenes the Prime Minister, Stanley Baldwin, and the King debated the options in the autumn, with the King clearly determined to marry.

There was indeed a limit to how long such a major story could be kept secret, though its first public appearance was tangential – on 30 November the Bishop of Bradford, in an address on the coronation, asked people

to commend him [the King] to God's grace, which he will so abundantly need . . . if he is to do his duty faithfully. We hope that he is aware of his need. Some of us wish that he gave more positive signs of such awareness.

^

King Edward VIII broadcasts his abdication speech to the nation on 11 December 1936.

The press saw this as a criticism of the King's relationship with Wallis Simpson and the scandal became public. The opposition to the King was almost universal and on 10 December 1936 he signed the abdication papers, left the country and then was created Duke of Windsor. The Duke of York became King George VI, a name selected to show some continuity with his father at this time of great crisis for the monarchy. In a week Elizabeth had gone from being a privileged schoolgirl to heir to the throne.

There were many changes in the lives of 'Us Four' once her father had become king, from moving into Buckingham Palace and Windsor Castle from the more domestic surroundings of 145 Piccadilly and the Royal Lodge, through to the formality of the court and greater involvement in the great occasions of state, most noticeably in the King's coronation on 12 May 1937, the date originally set aside for the coronation of his brother. However, Crawfie remained as a permanent fixture in the princesses' lives, Queen Mary continued to interest herself in their education and the King and Queen still ensured the absolute importance of time for the four of them to be together, in spite of all the new demands on them.

^
A souvenir postcard of the coronation.

World War II

The storm clouds were gathering over Europe, however. The brief hope engendered by prime minister Neville Chamberlain's Munich agreement with Hitler of 1938 and his message of 'peace in our time' quickly faded and, after the German invasion of Poland, Britain declared war on 3 September 1939. The King was to become a vital part of the war effort as the leader of his people and his first act was to make a solemn radio address on the day war was declared:

The task will be hard. There may be dark days ahead, and war can no longer be confined to the battlefield.

He saw that it was important that he and the Queen should be positively seen to be leading by example. Though they lived at Windsor Castle for most of the time, they worked from Buckingham Palace (which suffered bomb damage) and their visits to see the victims of the blitz endeared the King and Queen to the nation – indeed the combination of the dutiful and caring monarch and, from 1940, the pugnacious Winston Churchill as prime minister provided a wartime leadership of the nation that took the country through to the celebrations on VE Day and VJ Day in 1945.

The princesses stayed at Windsor for almost all the duration of the war, continuing their education and looking after their 'Dig

^
King George VI inspecting an Army division in the Southern Command, April 1940.

for Victory' allotment garden. Elizabeth's first public speech, with a little assistance from Margaret, was in a radio broadcast made on 13 October 1940 to the children of the Commonwealth and especially to children who had been evacuated within Britain or overseas, in which she concluded:

I can truthfully say to you all that we children at home are full of cheerfulness and courage. We are trying to do all we can to help our gallant sailors, soldiers and airmen, and we are trying, too, to bear our own share of the danger and sadness of war.

As the war progressed her father began to introduce her to the tasks of a monarch; on her sixteenth birthday in 1942 she became Honorary Colonel of the Grenadier Guards and two years later became Counsellor of State, empowered to act for her father in certain matters when he was absent. Elizabeth also wanted a more active role and towards the end of the war, against some family opposition, she trained with the Auxiliary Territorial Service (ATS), learning how to drive army lorries and how to look after them. Towards the end of March 1945 pictures of her, participating in a standard training course, show her delight in doing a practical job. VE Day on 8 May, celebrating victory in Europe, followed quickly after and, while the princess appeared in her ATS uniform on the balcony of Buckingham Palace during the day, she and some friends later went out into the streets of London to celebrate, and were in the crowds around Buckingham Palace in the evening shouting for the King.

Prince Philip of Greece

Britain entered a period of austerity as it recovered from the great costs of the war. For Elizabeth, however, romance played an important part in those immediate post-war years. Just before the war she had met Prince Philip of Greece at Dartmouth Naval College. Then aged 18, he showed off to the two visiting

1. Princess Elizabeth with Princess Margaret making her first radio broadcast in 1940; 2. Inspecting the Grenadier Guards at Windsor Castle on her sixteenth birthday, 1942; 3. Second subaltern in the ATS, 1945; 4. Helping her father with his official Red Boxes, at Windsor Castle, 1942; 5. Receiving a visit from her mother while undergoing her ATS training in 1945; 6. The Royal family and Winston Churchill celebrating the end of World War II in Europe, 8 May 1945 on the balcony at Buckingham Palace (with its window still boarded up to protect it from bombs). >

princesses. Philip was on the edge of the Royal family – his father was Prince Andrew of Greece, a second cousin to George VI, and his mother was Princess Alice of Battenberg (Lord Mountbatten's sister and great-granddaughter of Queen Victoria). However, the life of impoverished European royalty between the wars was not easy – Philip was born in Corfu in 1921, but the following year his family was exiled from Greece. He was brought up outside Paris, but by 1930 his parents had separated. His sisters, all significantly older than him, had married German princes and Philip attended a school run by the controversial teacher Kurt Hahn, first in Germany and then, when Hahn fled the Nazis, at Gordonstoun, which he established in northeastern Scotland in 1934 and where Philip was the school's third pupil.

His uncle, Lord Mountbatten, took him under his wing in 1938 and arranged for him to train at Dartmouth and then to enter the British Navy. He served with distinction in World War II and was able to spend Christmas 1943 at Windsor Castle (and to see Elizabeth perform in the castle's Christmas pantomime). After the war Elizabeth and Philip continued to meet. There was some disquiet within the British establishment, who felt that an English aristocrat rather than minor European royalty would be more appropriate, but Elizabeth's parents could see that he made their daughter very happy. Before the romance could develop further there were pressing Royal matters to attend to, with a trip to South Africa.

South Africa 1947

The Royal trip of 'Us Four' to South Africa was Elizabeth's first overseas trip. They set sail on 1 February 1947 on HMS *Vanguard* for a storm-tossed journey to South Africa, arriving on 17 February. Their trip was to last over two months, with a long tour around the country and an opportunity for the princesses to enjoy the wide open spaces and a relaxed style of life that was just not possible in austerity Britain. The trip also included one of the most important speeches Elizabeth has ever made, marking the occasion of her 21st birthday on 21 April 1947. In the speech she reflected upon the community of the Commonwealth and the future responsibilities that rested on the post-war generation:

If we all go forward together with an unwavering faith, a high courage, and a quiet heart, we shall be able to make of this ancient commonwealth, which we all love so dearly, an even grander thing – more free, more prosperous, more happy and a more powerful influence for good in the world – than it has been in the greatest days of our forefathers. . . .

I declare before you all that my whole life whether it be long or short shall be devoted to your service and the service of our great imperial family to which we all belong. But I shall not have strength to carry out this resolution alone unless you join in it with me, as I now invite you to do: I know that your support will be unfailingly given. God help me to make good my vow, and God bless all of you who are willing to share in it.

The Royal Wedding

Once the Royal party returned home, it was more romantic matters that occupied the Princess. On 10 July 1947 her engagement to Prince Philip was announced, with the wedding to be held on 20 November 1947 in Westminster Abbey. This being the wedding of the heir to the throne, a large and formal occasion was planned. Presents arrived from all over the world and heads of state and royalty were invited (with a few notable exceptions, for there were no invitations to Philip's three surviving sisters, who had all married German princes, nor for Elizabeth's uncle, the Duke of Windsor). It was, however, the largest gathering of European royalty for many years, though many of these notables now lived in rather lesser circumstances than they were once accustomed to. As the day approached there was fevered speculation over the wedding dress, designed by Norman Hartnell in ivory silk and lace and encrusted with small pearls. This speculation was not just over what the dress would look like, but also how many clothing coupons it would require and how British were its raw materials (a matter raised with the Palace by the Prime Minister's office). Ahead of the wedding Prince Philip was given the titles of Duke of Edinburgh, Baron Greenwich and Earl of Merioneth.

On a dry and not-too-cold November day, crowds lined the route from Buckingham Palace to the Abbey and the service was broadcast live on the radio and listened to by millions around the world. A film was also made and shown on the evening of the wedding day in cinemas around Britain. It was a major celebration and marked a distinct increase of interest by the general public in such events, which had previously, for the most part, been more low key. It became one of the first international Royal events, benefiting from the use of radio, film and a little television. *The Times* became overwhelmed by the day, commenting that 'this was a family event, transacted in the bosom of history'.

The Young Family

Around a year later there were family celebrations marking the birth of Prince Charles, on 14 November 1948 at Buckingham

^
Princess Elizabeth and the Duke of Edinburgh on their wedding day, surrounded by their family and members of other European Royal families.

Palace. He was christened Charles Philip Arthur George at Buckingham Palace on 15 December. In the summer of 1949 the new Royal family was finally able to move into Clarence House, by St James's Palace, after its long period of restoration from bomb damage and neglect. Elizabeth became more involved in learning about matters of state while Philip continued his naval career and in October he took over as second in command of HMS *Chequers*, based in Malta. Elizabeth joined him for a month over Christmas, leaving Charles to spend Christmas at Sandringham.

On 15 August of the following year Princess Anne was born at Clarence House and was christened Anne Elizabeth Alice Louise at Buckingham Palace on 21 October, after which the Duke of Edinburgh returned to his command of HMS *Magpie* in Malta. In a move that might now cause surprise, Elizabeth followed him in late November, spending two-and-a-half months in Malta while the children remained with their grandparents. But the time for such relaxation was drawing to a close. George VI was not in good health and Elizabeth was having to undertake more duties on his behalf, such as attending the Trooping the Colour in 1951. By September George's doctors knew that he had lung cancer though, reflecting medical practice at the time, they did not make this public. In the autumn Elizabeth and Philip flew to Canada and the USA for an official visit, the first time members of the Royal family had flown across the Atlantic. In Canada the Duke was relaxed but Elizabeth was rather stiffer, no doubt greatly concerned by the health of her father, but she had relaxed by the time they reached Washington DC, where she completely won over President Truman, who remarked, 'When I was a little boy, I read about a fairy princess, and there she is.' Once they had returned to London it was clear that her father would not be able to undertake a major royal tour planned for the following year, so Elizabeth and Philip prepared to set off on a five-month tour early in 1952, stating first with a visit to Kenya and then on to Ceylon and Australia.

The Queen's Accession and Coronation

Queen Elizabeth II after her coronation in Westminster Abbey, London, 2 June 1953.

The Queen's Accession and Coronation

Princess Elizabeth starts an overseas tour

On 31 January 1952, Princess Elizabeth and the Duke of Edinburgh headed for London Airport for the start of a five-month overseas tour that was to begin with a trip to Kenya, giving them a chance to stay in their wedding present from the colonial government, a forest lodge in the foothills of Mount Kenya. The family came to see them off, with George VI making his first public appearance since September 1951. In an emotional newsreel report of the departure, he looks gaunt and thin, and all-too-aware that he might never see his elder daughter again.

The couple arrived in Nairobi the next day, undertaking various official functions. They also visited Nairobi National Park, with Princess Elizabeth recording the scene with a cine camera. Probably the most unimpressed animal they met was a lion, according to the report in *The Times*:

^
King George VI waving farewell to the plane carrying Princess Elizabeth and the Duke of Edinburgh to Kenya in January 1952.

As they turned a corner they came upon a magnificent lion under a tree eating a wildebeest it had killed that morning. The lion looked up and advanced several paces. It stopped, yawned, and then turned and went back under the tree and lay down watching the Princess as she photographed it.

Next they travelled 100 miles north to stay in their wedding present, Sagana Lodge, near Nyeri. A highlight of their stay was to be a night spent in the Treetops lodge in the Aberdare National Park. Treetops at that time consisted of a four-room treehouse resting in the boughs of an ancient ficus tree overlooking a much-visited animal watering hole. It had been redecorated for the Royal visit, but nature still ruled the area – some baboons had got inside and eaten some of the new lampshades.

Treetops lodge. In his book *Tree Tops*, Jim Corbett, embroidering the events wrote that 'For the first time in the history of the world, a young woman climbed into a tree a princess, and after having what she described as her most thrilling experience, she climbed down from the tree the next day a queen – God bless her.'

To provide extra protection the party was escorted by Jim Corbett, renowned in India as a hunter, naturalist and early conservationist, who had moved to Nyeri from India in 1947. During the night the Royal couple watched animals in the moonlight coming to the waterhole to drink and, tired but exhilarated, they left Treetops at 9 o'clock the next morning and headed back to Sagana Lodge.

THE DEATH OF GEORGE VI

They did not know that George VI had died in his sleep at Sandringham that night and that Elizabeth was now queen. Indeed news only began to filter through around 2 o'clock in the afternoon, when the Princess's private secretary, then in Nyeri, was asked by a journalist if he could comment on the news. Three-quarters of an hour later, the news was officially confirmed and the Duke of Edinburgh told his wife at Sagana Lodge that her father had died and that she was now queen. Within three hours the Royal party was at Nanyuki airfield, and a small plane took the Queen and the Duke of Edinburgh to Entebbe in Uganda, from where they flew to London, arriving on the afternoon of 7 February, a week since they had left Britain.

The Queen was met at the airport by the Prime Minister, Winston Churchill, and other senior figures. From the airport the Royal couple travelled to Clarence House, the Queen knowing that she had first to attend to matters of state (and particularly to the Declaration of Accession that she was to make the following day). Following her Declaration, she travelled to Sandringham to be with her children and her mother, whom she had not yet seen since her return.

The Queen arriving at London Airport on 7 February 1952 on her return from Kenya. She is being met by Lord Woolton, Anthony Eden, Clement Atlee and Winston Churchill.

The coffin of King George VI being taken off the train at King's Cross Station to be taken to Westminster Hall for the Lying-in-State.

The King's coffin was brought by train to London on 11 February for three days of lying in state in Westminster Hall, during which time over 300,000 people paid their personal tribute to the King. On Friday 15 February the funeral procession left Westminster at 9.30 in the morning, just as Big Ben began to toll 56 times, marking the age of the King at his death. His coffin, draped in the Royal Standard, with the Imperial Crown and other regalia and a white wreath from the Queen Mother on top, was placed on a gun carriage. It was then pulled by sailors from the Royal Navy at the head of a funeral procession that was over one mile long, led by family mourners and followed by representatives of other Royal families, heads of state and military contingents from Britain, the Commonwealth and many other countries. It made its way from Westminster to Paddington Station for the journey to Windsor and the funeral service in St George's Chapel within Windsor Castle, where the King was buried.

^
The gun carriage with the coffin of King George VI passing through Piccadilly on its way from Westminster to Paddington Station.

The Accession

The formal process of Accession started with a brief announcement from Buckingham Palace:

It was announced from Sandringham at 10.45 a.m. today, February 6, 1952, that the King, who retired to rest last night in his usual health, passed peacefully away in his sleep early this morning.

Whilst the Queen became monarch immediately upon the death of her father, there were various legal requirements to be performed. The Accession Council, made up of members of the Privy Council, representatives of Commonwealth countries and the Lord Mayor and Aldermen of the City of London, met on the evening of 6 February at St James's Palace. They approved and signed the Proclamation of Accession, in which they

...do now hereby with one Voice and Consent of Tongue and Heart publish and proclaim, That the High and Mighty Princess Elizabeth Alexandra Mary is now, by the Death of our late Sovereign of happy Memory, become Queen Elizabeth the Second, by the Grace of God, Queen of this Realm, and of Her other Realms and Territories, Head of the Commonwealth, Defender of the Faith, to whom Her Lieges do acknowledge all Faith and constant Obedience with hearty and humble Affection, beseeching God by whom Kings and Queens do reign, to bless the Royal Princess Elizabeth the Second with long and happy Years to reign over us. God save the Queen.

On the morning of 8 February the Queen attended the Accession Council at St James's Palace, at which she made her Declaration of Accession and a separate oath to maintain and preserve the Church of Scotland, a stipulation going back to the 1707 Act of Union.

The Declaration of Accession

By the sudden death of my dear father I am called to assume the duties and responsibilities of sovereignty. At this time of deep sorrow, it is a profound consolation to me to be assured of the sympathy which you and all my peoples feel towards me, to my mother and my sister, and to other members of my family.

My father was our revered and beloved head, as he was of the wider family of his subjects: the grief which his loss brings is shared among us all. My heart is too full for me to say more to you today than that I shall always work as my father did throughout his reign, to uphold constitutional government and to advance the happiness and prosperity of my peoples, spread as they are all the world over.

I know that in my resolve to follow his shining example of service and devotion I shall be inspired by the loyalty and affection of those whose queen I have been called to be, and by the counsel of their elected Parliaments.

I pray that God will help me discharge worthily this heavy task that has been laid upon me so early in my life.

The Proclamation of Accession was then publically read out, first at St James's Palace, then at Charing Cross, Temple Bar and the Royal Exchange in London and in cities, towns and villages across the country.

Amongst the titles of the Queen was one which had never before appeared in a Proclamation of Accession, and that was 'Head of the Commonwealth', a title created in 1947 as the period of post-war decolonization began. India and Pakistan became independent republics, but she retained the honoured position of

'Head of the Commonwealth', as was recognized in a message from Jawaharlal Nehru, prime minister of India:

In Your Majesty's bereavement you have the deepest sympathy of innumerable people in this country. May I also welcome Your Majesty as the new head of the Commonwealth and earnestly trust that this great fellowship will continue to work for the cause of human understanding and peace throughout the world.

^
The Lancaster Herald reads the Proclamation of Accession of Queen Elizabeth II from a royal carriage at Charing Cross in central London, 8 February 1952.

Preparing for the Coronation

After the burial of the King, minds began to turn to the coronation of the new Queen, which was fixed for 2 June 1953. This gave plenty of time for making all the formal arrangements, but it also created a period of expectation that developed over the sixteen months from the Accession to make the Coronation a moment of national celebration on a scale not seen before.

Since her father's coronation in 1937 the new medium of television had been developed and there was much debate in the lead up to the Coronation as to what role television should play in the event. Initially the cameras were only going to record events outside Westminster Abbey and not the solemn events within (so solemn that some clergy felt that it would be inappropriate for people to watch while drinking cups of tea or pints of beer). However, there was much unfavourable reaction to this decision and the Queen, it is thought, subsequently encouraged the authorities to allow the service to be televised. This broadcast had a remarkable impact, for it was estimated that 27 million people in Britain watched the Coronation, with more viewing it in France, Germany, Holland and the USA. The relationships between the monarchy, the people and the media were changed forever, as people realized that they could now be a part of Royal ceremonies and would in the future expect the monarchy to be much more publically visible than before.

^
Flag makers preparing for the Coronation.

Coronation Day

As 2 June approached, the streets of London were transformed by great decorations, including enormous decorative metal arches over The Mall, by stands of seating along parts of the processional route and by hundreds of thousands of people descending on the capital. On the night of 1 June, an unseasonably damp and cool night, over half a million people camped on the streets, warmed by the news in the early hours that Edmund Hillary and Norkey Tenzing were the first people to reach the summit of Mount Everest. The day itself was overcast with some rain, but not enough to dampen the spirits of the spectators and the millions more up and down the country who were preparing for street parties and village celebrations.

The Queen's coach arrived at Westminster Abbey at 11 o'clock and she then processed into the Abbey for the start of the Coronation service. The origins of the service and its symbolism go back to the coronation of King Edgar in Bath in 973. However, it is inextricably linked to Westminster Abbey, which has been the setting of virtually every coronation since William the Conqueror in 1066. The service was led by the Archbishop of Canterbury, Geoffrey Fisher, and took place within the context of the Holy Communion service of the Church of England, of which the Queen is the Supreme Governor.

At the start of the service, the Queen took the coronation oath in which she assented to various questions, posed to her by the Archbishop, to govern her peoples according to their respective laws, to cause 'Law and Justice, in Mercy, to be executed in all your judgements', and to maintain the 'Laws of God and the true profession of the Gospel'. After this her outer crimson robe was removed and she sat in the Coronation Chair,

1. Crowds greet the Gold State Coach as it leaves Buckingham Palace for the coronation at Westminster Abbey; > *2. The Queen arriving at Westminster Abbey for the coronation service. 3. The Queen after she was crowned with St Edward's Crown, wearing the golden coronation robes and holding the sceptre with cross, representing her temporal powers, and the sceptre with dove, representing equity and mercy; 4. The Archbishop of Canterbury places St Edward's Crown on the Queen's head. 5. The new Queen and her consort Prince Philip, wave to crowds from the balcony of Buckingham Palace.*

1

2

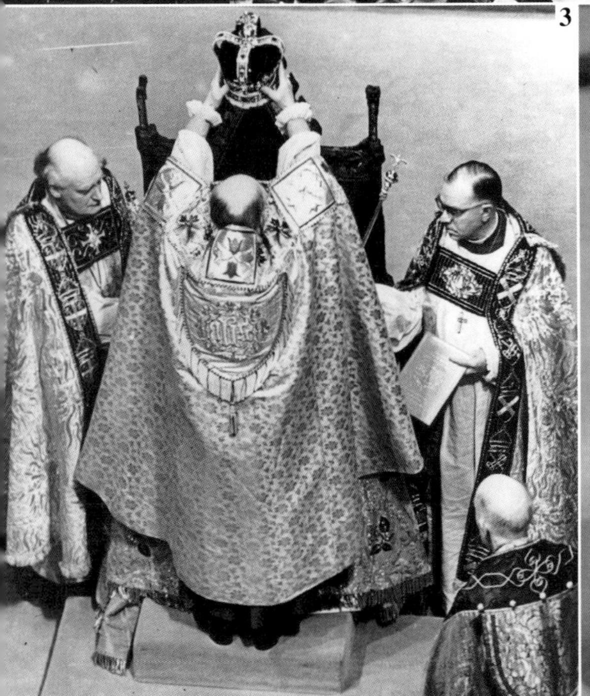

3

4

5

made for Edward I and incorporating the Stone of Scone, and was anointed with holy oil by the Archbishop, consecrating her for the duties of the sovereign. Then she was dressed in golden robes and received the Royal Regalia, symbols of her authority, chivalry, wisdom, justice and mercy. Finally St Edward's Crown, originally made for Charles II and based on the design of Edward the Confessor's crown, was placed on her head by the Archbishop. At the end of the service, the Queen went to St Edward's Chapel to re-emerge in purple robes and wearing the Imperial State Crown. This crown was made for her father based on a crown used by Queen Victoria. Set into the cross on top of the crown is a sapphire that belonged to Edward the Confessor.

She then processed out of the Abbey for the start of the Coronation Procession around the streets of London, joined by dignitaries and over 20,000 troops and marching bands, to great acclamation from an estimated three million people lining the damp streets. The procession finally made its way down The Mall and back to Buckingham Palace. She and Prince Philip then appeared on the Palace's balcony in front of the great throng of people who now filled The Mall.

At the end of the day the Queen broadcast a message from Buckingham Palace, and concluded with these words: 'As this day draws to its close, I know that my abiding memory of it will be, not only the solemnity and beauty of the ceremony, but the inspiration of your loyalty and affection. I thank you all from a full heart. God bless you all.' And finally at 11.30 p.m. the Queen and Prince Philip went out once again onto the balcony and spent three minutes waving to the crowd of 30,000 who had waited in drizzling rain for a last chance to see the Queen before the end of her Coronation Day.

Queen Elizabeth II holding the orb, symbolizing Christian rule of the world and the sceptre symbolizing her temporal power, against a backdrop of Henry VII's Chapel at Westminster Abbey. >

The First Decade 1952-1961

The Queen at Benares during her tour of India in 1961.

The First Decade 1952–1961

From the moment of her accession the Queen became monarch of the nation. Even before her coronation on 2 June 1953, there were matters of state to attend to including annual events such as Trooping the Colour in June, the Remembrance Day ceremony at the Cenotaph in November and regular State Openings of Parliament. The decade saw the Queen's family grow, her sister marry and the nation move from rationing to the time when we 'never had it so good', in the words of the then prime minster, Harold Macmillan.

^
The Queen, the Duke of Edinburgh and the Duke of Gloucester at the Remembrance Day ceremony at the Cenotaph on 9 November 1952.

The Royal Family

Queen Mary had seen her granddaughter become the new monarch but she was not able to witness her coronation, for she died on 24 March 1953 at the age of 85. She had had a significant influence on the education of her granddaughter and was the embodiment of the continuity of the Royal family, having married George V in 1893. Her funeral took place in St George's Chapel in Windsor after a formal period of lying in state in Westminster Hall. Before her death she had insisted that no period of mourning should delay the Coronation.

The move of the Queen and her family into Buckingham Palace also meant that the Queen Mother, widowed when only fifty-one, needed to move out of the Palace. Princess Margaret moved with the Queen Mother to Clarence House, which would remain the Queen Mother's London home for the next fifty years.

The death of her father and the changed position of her sister had made Princess Margaret, usually so outgoing, rather withdrawn. She sought companionship from Group Captain Peter Townsend, her father's former equerry and now equerry and comptroller of the Queen Mother's household. He was sixteen years older than Princess Margaret and was the innocent party in a divorce from his wife in 1952. One small gesture at the Coronation, where Princess Margaret gently brushed some fluff off his uniform, was immediately picked up by the American press and soon featured in the British press also, and much speculation ensued. Legally the Queen had to approve any proposed marriage of her sister before her twenty-fifth birthday and she had already indicated that, if asked, she would not give her approval. While Margaret was on a Royal trip to the Caribbean, Townsend was posted as air attaché to the embassy in Brussels, effectively exiled. They remained in regular contact, however, and as Princess Margaret's twenty-fifth birthday approached, speculation mounted as to what they might do. The Archbishop of Canterbury and the establishment remained opposed to the idea of a marriage, whilst popular sentiment was on the side of the princess. The establishment view was trenchantly put forward in a leader in *The Times*:

The Royal family is above all things the symbol and guarantee of the unity of the British peoples; if one of its members herself becomes a cause for division, the salt has lost its savour.

Princess Margaret and Peter Townsend reluctantly fell in with the establishment view and ended their relationship, but not before there had been great press interest in the story, with journalists and photographers stalking both of them. It was an early example of the press's difficult relationship with the Palace.

There was, however, no establishment opposition in 1959 when the engagement of Princess Margaret to the Royal photographer and old Etonian, Antony Armstrong-Jones, was announced. The wedding took place at Westminster Abbey on 6 May 1960, a fine late spring day, and was the first Royal wedding to be televised. The groom was given the title Earl of Snowdon in 1961.

Princess Margaret and Antony Armstrong-Jones at Buckingham Palace after their wedding in May 1960.

Prince Charles and Princess Anne were brought up at Buckingham Palace, and spent much time in the company of their Scottish nanny, Mabel Anderson, who had joined what was then Princess Elizabeth's household in 1949 (and remained with the Royal family until 1982). In 1956, Prince Charles was sent to Hill House pre-preparatory school in Knightsbridge, the first heir to the throne to have been sent to a school rather than educated privately. After one year he moved to Cheam preparatory school (his father's old school), and then to Gordonstoun in 1962.

^
The Queen with Prince Charles and Princess Anne in 1952.

There was great celebration on 19 February 1960, when the Queen gave birth to Prince Andrew Albert Christian Edward, the first child born at Buckingham Palace into a monarch's family since Princess Beatrice was born in 1857. Just ahead of Prince Andrew's birth, the government agreed that, while the dynasty would still be called the House of Windsor, members of the immediate Royal family would have the surname Mountbatten-Windsor, rather than just Windsor, an issue that had concerned the Duke of Edinburgh since his wife became Queen.

Whilst the Queen was familiar with the more formal nature of the Palace and its courtiers, Prince Philip was less at home and found it difficult to adapt to these new surroundings, though he was able to influence some reforms, such as arranging a series of more informal lunches at the Palace for people with a wide range of interests. He encouraged the first televised Christmas broadcast in 1957 (and wrote the final draft), which was transmitted live

^
The Royal family at Balmoral in September 1960.

from Sandringham, and was pleased to see the ending of the presentations of debutantes to court, last held in 1958. He also encouraged the idea that the traditional Maundy service on the Thursday before Easter, at which the Queen gives Maundy coins to an equal number of male and female pensioners (the number being the Queen's age) should not just be held at Westminster Abbey but also at cathedrals and abbeys around the country.

The Queen's enthusiasm for horses bore fruit during her first decade on the throne. On Derby Day, just four days after the Coronation, her horse Aureole came second in the Derby, and in both 1954 and 1957 she was the leading racehorse owner in Britain in terms of prize winnings. The interest still continues but her success has never matched those early years.

The Queen leads her horse Carrozza, ridden by Lester Piggott, after winning The Oaks at Epsom in 1957.

The Queen in Britain

One of her first formal acts was the State Opening of Parliament on 4 November 1952. It is one of the most significant constitutional events in the British political calendar and one taken most seriously by the Queen. Only twice in her reign (in both cases when she was pregnant) has she missed the occasion, and she has taken part in more State Openings than any other monarch. The basic purpose of the State Opening is for the monarch to open a new session of Parliament and to outline the policies and plans of her government for the next year. Though delivered by the Queen, the speech is actually written by the government of the day. Although she is Head of State, she can give no opinions nor influence the contents of the speech, a peculiarly British constitutional solution to the sometimes strained relations that there once were between monarch and parliament. Her first opening was much commented on, from the clear and confident delivery of the speech, to an almost excessive interest in her clothes and looks from the likes of Cecil Beaton.

Towards the end of June 1953 the Queen travelled to Scotland. In Edinburgh there was a National Service of Thanksgiving to celebrate the Coronation, and to mark the occasion the 'Honours of Scotland', the crown jewels of Scotland, which date from the 15th and 16th centuries, were taken in state through the streets of Edinburgh to St Giles Cathedral and presented to the Queen. She wrote to Churchill that the 'Scottish capital was thrilled by all the pageantry' (though some felt she should be called Elizabeth I in Scotland, because Scotland had its own monarchy when Elizabeth I ruled England). This was not her first Royal visit to Scotland, because she had been at the John Brown shipyard at Clydebank on 16 April 1953 to launch the Royal Yacht *Britannia*, which was to become a regular part of Royal life. The Queen also made a coronation trip to Wales in July, complete with a ceremony in the great castle of Caernarfon.

As monarch, the Queen holds regular private audiences with the Prime Minister. Initially they were with the familiar figure of Winston Churchill, who was charmed by the new Queen. But Churchill, who reached the age of 80 in 1954, was no longer in good health and announced his resignation in 1955. It was the duty of the Queen to ask his successor to form a new government, a straightforward process if there was a clear successor. On this occasion, there was Sir Anthony Eden, but two years later, Eden resigned and there were two potential candidates within the Conservative Party. It thus fell to the Queen to select either Harold Macmillan or R.A. Butler. Her advisers, however, left it to the party hierarchy to make a recommendation (Macmillan), but there was much embarrassment that the Queen was put in this position.

The Queen's Royal duties in Britain took her to many parts of the country in her first decade on the throne. The optimism of the age is reflected in her October 1956 visit to the Cumbrian coast to open Calder Hall, the world's first large-scale nuclear power station. There was great hope for this new technology with the Queen noting that: 'this new power which has proved itself to be such a terrifying weapon of destruction, is harnessed for the first time for the common good of our community'.

^
The Queen and Sir Winston Churchill, with Prince Charles and Princess Anne in the foreground.

^
The Queen officiates at the opening of the world's first nuclear power station at Calder Hall in 1956.

The Queen around the World

When the Queen came to the throne, the British Empire had been in the process of changing irreversibly, first with the independence, as republics within the Commonwealth, of India and Pakistan in 1947, and of Burma in 1948 outside the Commonwealth. The African colony of the Gold Coast was the first British colony in Africa to become independent, as Ghana, in 1957, and many more followed in the next decade; the 'wind of change is blowing through this continent' as Harold Macmillan described it in a speech in South Africa in 1960.

The Queen's first major overseas visit in 1953-4 was before these changes, however. It was a round-the-world journey starting in Bermuda on 24 November 1953 followed by Jamaica and Panama and over the Pacific via Fiji and Tonga to the main attraction, nearly three months spent in Australia and New Zealand. Wherever she went, huge numbers of people came out to see her, from city centres to small railway stops in the Australian outback. Never again would a tour generate such a response – in Australia and New Zealand it was the first time that a ruling monarch had visited, and the governments and people made sure they put on a show. The Queen and the Duke of Edinburgh returned via Ceylon, Aden, Uganda, and Malta, finally reaching Gibraltar on 10 May 1954. The Royal Yacht *Britannia*, on its maiden voyage, brought Prince Charles and Princess Anne to Gibraltar to meet them, and the family returned to Britain on *Britannia*, passing through Tower Bridge on 15 May, and bringing to an end a journey of 43,618 miles.

The Queen's role as Head of State was clearly shown in her first official visit to the USA in October 1957. The Queen and the Duke of Edinburgh stayed at the White House with

1. The Queen and the Duke of Edinburgh leaving the House of Assembly in Hamilton, Bermuda, at the start of their 1953–4 tour; 2. The Queen, Queen Salote Tupou III of Tonga and the Duke of Edinburgh watching a tortoise presented to the Tongan Royal family by Captain Cook; 3. The Queen arrives at Farm Cove in Sydney on 3 February 1954 and becomes the first ruling British monarch to set foot in Australia; 4. The Royal Yacht Britannia brings the Queen back to London at the end of her tour.

1

2

3

4

President Eisenhower and attended a round of official banquets and receptions. The Royal couple also went to see an American football match, following which *The Times* reported that 'she looked a little puzzled' while on the way back from the game they made an unexpected stop 'at a suburban "super market", where they chatted with astonished Saturday shoppers and saw something of the American way of buying a week's supplies under one roof' as the paper reported. Following four days in Washington, they travelled to New York, welcomed with a ticker-tape parade in Manhattan and a trip to the top of the Empire State Building. In between this and two massive receptions, each with over 4,000 guests, she also addressed the General Assembly of the United Nations in which she concluded 'When justice and respect for obligations are firmly established the United Nations will the more confidently achieve the goal of a world at peace, law-abiding and prosperous, for which men and women have striven so long and which is the heart's desire of every nation here represented.' It was to be over 50 years before she again addressed the Assembly.

As the decade progressed, her overseas tours had become more focused on her role as the Head of the Commonwealth. At the start of 1961, she made the first official visit to India and Pakistan as Head of the Commonwealth. The tour of India started with a visit to the memorial to Mahatma Gandhi and mixed the traditional (a moonlit visit to the Taj Mahal, riding on elephants, taking part in a tiger hunt organized by the Maharajah of Jaipur, and going to the races in Calcutta) along with the modern (visiting factories, technical institutes and India's atomic energy establishment). She also spent time in Pakistan, visiting the tomb of Muhammad Ali Jinnah, the father of the nation, and seeing both modern and historic sites. At the start of the trip, the Queen stopped in Cyprus, the first visit by a British monarch since 1191 when Richard I visited, according to *The Times*. Sometimes the Queen must wish to escape from her ancestors.

In November 1961 she made an historic trip to West Africa, primarily to Ghana, which became independent in 1957 and had declared itself a republic in 1960. The rule of Dr Nkrumah had become increasingly repressive and there was concern in London over whether it was safe for the Queen to visit. Such difficult choices inevitably come to the Head of the Commonwealth and the Queen felt that the invitation given by Ghana should be honoured. The visit duly went ahead and there was an infectious welcome from the people of Ghana, although there was some tension in relations with Nkrumah himself. A memorable image from the trip was of the Queen dancing with Nkrumah at an official ball, an image that shocked the apartheid government in South Africa, which had resigned from the Commonwealth in May 1961.

^
The Queen at Delhi polo ground during her Indian tour in 1961.

The Second Decade 1962–1971

The Queen presenting the World Cup to England's captain, Bobby Moore, after England had beaten Germany 4–2 in the 1966 World Cup final.

The Second Decade 1962–1971

This was a decade of great change in Britain. It came with increased economic confidence, the growth of the permissive society and challenges to the established order, whether from the satirist's pen or the revolution in popular music. As the position of the Establishment was challenged, so the importance of the monarchy to the British people decreased. In the late 1960s attempts were made to show the monarchy as being easier to relate to, most notably in *The Royal Family* television documentary, which presented the Royal family as an idealized 'normal' family.

The family

The decade saw the completion of the Queen's family, with the birth, on 10 March 1964, of Prince Edward Antony Richard Louis who was christened by the Dean of Windsor in the Private Chapel at Windsor Castle on 2 May. His first public appearance followed Trooping the Colour when the Queen carried him on to the balcony at Buckingham Palace.

^
Prince Edward makes his first public appearance alongside his mother, father, and a young Prince Andrew, on the Buckingham Palace balcony, after Trooping the Colour in June 1964.

Prince Charles and Princess Anne also emerged into the public domain. Prince Charles moved to Gordonstoun in 1962 and did not appear to enjoy the school's regime. In 1966 he went to Australia to spend two terms at Timbertop, an isolated outpost of Geelong Grammar School, in the foothills of the Great Dividing Range. Even when recalling the hardships of night hikes and other adventures, his verdict overall was that he loved it. He returned to Gordonstoun for a final year, took his A-levels and then went to Trinity College, Cambridge in October 1967, the first heir to the throne to attend university for a normal three-year period of study. He started studying archaeology and anthropology and then transferred to history.

The Queen had made him Prince of Wales in 1959 and ten years later he was formally invested with the title in a specially created event at Caernarfon Castle. The event was master-minded by Lord Snowdon and was arranged to make the most of the television potential of the occasion. In advance of the investiture, which took place on 1 July 1969, Prince Charles had spent a term at University College of Wales, Aberystwyth, gaining a limited knowledge of the Welsh language. The Investiture all went to plan (fears of disruption by Welsh separatists did not materialize) and in spite of the quaintness of the ceremony (as well as some less than kind remarks about the Queen's hat and the Prince of Wales's new coronet) it was widely seen as a success.

Princess Anne, after being educated in the Palace, started at Benenden School in Kent in 1963. She left in 1968 after taking A-levels but decided not to go to university, instead pursuing her passion and ability in horse-riding. In 1971 she won the European Three-Day Event held at Burghley, near Stamford in Lincolnshire, and later that year was Sportswoman of the Year and the BBC Sports Personality of 1971.

1

2

HALIFAX BUILDING SOCIETY

3

The private world of the Royal family was opened to public examination in 1969 when a documentary, *The Royal Family*, filmed over the course of the year, was first shown in June. It was then repeated a number of times and it was estimated that nearly 70 per cent of the country had seen it by the end of the year. Not only did the film show behind-the-scenes moments at official events, it also recorded the private family life of the Queen and her family, from discussions around the lunch table through to barbecues at Balmoral. The initial response was very favourable, reinforcing the Palace's wish to show that the members of the family had their own private personalities, making them appear less remote than they had been previously viewed. The sting, however, was slower burning, for if the Royal family were happy to show their personal life when recorded under their own terms, then the press would feel more relaxed in reporting less approved stories about them. The film was withdrawn by Buckingham Palace at the end of 1969 and has never been seen since.

^
A family lunch at Windsor Castle, as recorded for the documentary The Royal Family.

< *1. The Prince of Wales in his Investiture robes at Caernarfon Castle in July 1969; 2. The Queen with the Prince of Wales after the ceremony; 3. Princess Anne on her horse Doublet, on her way to winning the European Three Day Event in 1971.*

The Queen in Britain

In 1962 the Queen attended the consecration of Coventry Cathedral, built next to the ruins of the bomb-damaged medieval cathedral. The Queen had laid the foundation stone in 1956 and the building, designed by Sir Basil Spence, was seen as a symbol of post-war reconciliation, a process further reinforced in 1965 with the Queen's state visit to Germany and the state visit to Britain of Emperor Hirohito of Japan in 1971. This was, perhaps, the most sensitive of state visits that the Queen had hosted, as he had been Emperor since 1926 and he engendered strong emotions for many who had suffered at the hands of the Japanese during World War II.

After the difficulties around the appointment of Harold Macmillan as prime minister in 1957, it had been hoped that future appointments would happen more smoothly. However, in October 1963 Macmillan was taken ill and had to announce his intention to resign at a time when there were a number of contenders for the post. It was the Queen's prerogative to choose a successor, but who was to advise her on that choice? The Conservative Party had no mechanism in place to select a leader. In the end the Queen went to see Macmillan in hospital, accepted

^
The Queen with Emperor Hirohito during his state visit in 1971.

his resignation and then sought his advice. While R.A. Butler would have been the popular choice, Macmillan did not support him and recommended the Foreign Secretary, Lord Home. Duly advised, the Queen asked Lord Home to form a government, to the consternation of many, for he was the least favoured of the potential candidates and questions were asked about the Queen's decision-making process.

Lord Home, who resigned his peerage and became Sir Alec Douglas-Home, had an easy and unchallenging relationship with the Queen, with whom he shared many interests. His relationship with the country was less secure, however, and he was defeated in the 1964 general election, which was won by the Labour Party, nearly twenty years after their last victory. This signalled a major change in British politics, and courtiers at the Palace were most concerned about how the new prime minister, Harold Wilson, and the Queen would get on at the regular audiences. To their great surprise, they worked well together, and audiences, it was noted, grew longer. The Conservative Party that won the 1970 election was different from that of Macmillan and Home, and the new prime minister, Edward Heath, was not particularly interested

^
The Queen with her prime minister Harold Wilson in 1969.

in traditions of monarchy nor was he gracious, and audiences became formulaic. However, it was during his administration that the first increase of the 'Civil List' (the funding provided to the monarch by the state) since the Coronation, was agreed on terms viewed as satisfactory by the Palace.

The Honours system, whereby prominent individuals are awarded a range of honours by the monarch, was seen as a part of the Establishment. The Queen acts on the advice of the government for all the honours awarded (apart from the Order of Merit, which is in her personal gift). Thus it was in June 1965 that the four members of The Beatles were awarded the MBE and the investiture took place in October, not before a few disgruntled holders of awards had returned theirs to the Palace. The following year, the Queen played her part in England's great World Cup moment when she attended the final and presented the trophy to the England captain, Bobby Moore. As a further part of making the monarchy more open, the knighting of Francis Chichester, who was the first person to sail solo around the world, took place not within the confines of Buckingham Palace but at Greenwich, with the Queen using Sir Francis Drake's sword, an image designed for the front page of newspapers.

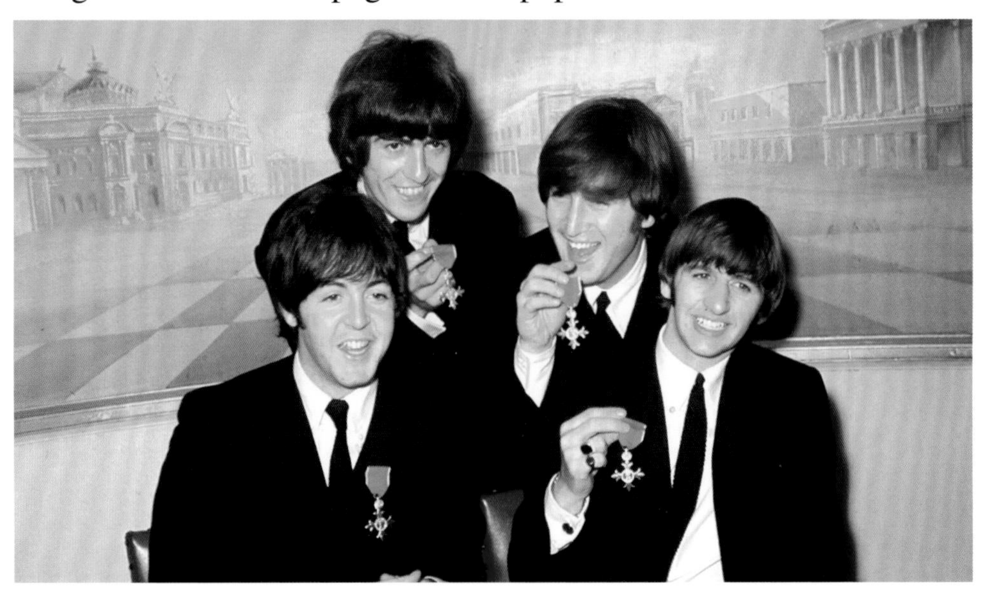

^
The Beatles, after they had received their MBEs from the Queen in October 1965.

Much more taxing was the response to the Aberfan disaster on 21 October 1966 after the Pantglas Junior School was overwhelmed by a landslide of mining waste that killed 144 people, 116 of whom were pupils at the school. While the Duke of Edinburgh and Lord Snowdon went the next day to Aberfan, the Queen held back, not wishing, she said, to get in the way of rescue workers. This might have seemed, in the eyes of the public, a miscalculation, but her visit a week later was a very moving affair. A Red Cross worker commented that 'The Queen seemed so near tears but she kept fighting them back. We all felt very close to her.' She was presented with a small posy of flowers, such a normal event on a Royal visit except this time the message on it read 'From the remaining children of Aberfan'. It was a dignified, sympathetic and affecting visit.

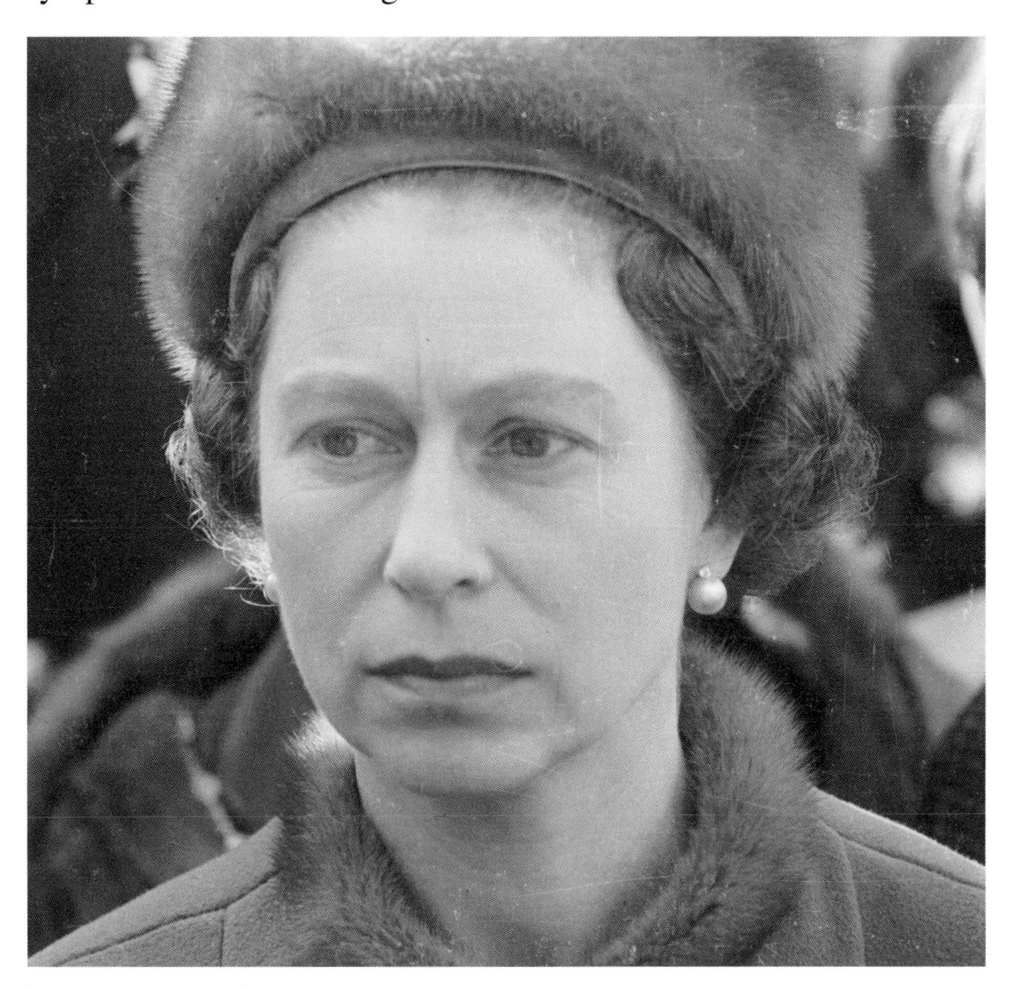

^
The Queen visiting Aberfan in October 1966.

The Queen around the World

This decade saw a major change in the nature of the Queen's formal status in many former colonies, for this was the time when many countries in Africa and the Caribbean became independent of Britain. They remained within the Commonwealth, some still retaining the Queen as Head of State and some becoming republics with only membership of the Commonwealth linking them with Britain. The Queen herself did not attend any of the ceremonies where independence was formally granted, but many members of the Royal family did – the Duke of Edinburgh was in Nairobi for the granting of independence to Kenya under the leadership of Jomo Kenyatta in 1963, for example.

As well as visits to Commonwealth countries (sometimes now brief and linked to a particular occasion), the Queen was making (on the advice of her government), an increasing number of state visits to countries that did not necessarily have any traditional links with Britain – for example visits to Brazil and Chile in 1968. In 1965 she made two significant trips; the first, in February, to Ethiopia and the Sudan, and the second to West Germany.

In Ethiopia, the Royal party was welcomed by Emperor Haile Selaisse, ruler of Ethiopia since 1930. After a few days in Addis Ababa they travelled to see the source of the Blue Nile and then on to Gondar, a former capital, where they stayed in a compound of 50 tents, not the usual accommodation for a state visit. There can be little doubt that the Emperor relished the Queen's gift of a thoroughbred racehorse (though its name of Robespierre may have surprised some). At a final banquet the Queen returned the crown and seal of King Theodore, looted by British troops in 1868, an act greatly appreciated. The trip then continued to Sudan, a trip of some uncertainty as General Abboud, who had invited the Queen, had since been overthrown. The reception in Khartoum was 'boisterous' according to *The Times*, and among the visits was one to the camel races at Khartoum Racing Club.

Of a very different nature was the state visit to West Germany in May 1965, a state occasion the like of which had not been seen since before 1914. There was immense German interest and the tour culminated with a visit to the then divided city of Berlin, where the Queen was met by enthusiastic crowds (including 500 East Berliners who watched from behind the Wall). The German Chancellor spoke, prophetically, that the visit had strengthened German hopes of an end to the division of their country and that the wish for unity and self-determination could never be stilled in view of the 'wall of tyranny'.

A revolution in the perception of Royal visits happened during the Queen's 1970 tour to New Zealand. In Wellington, as the Royal party headed towards the City Hall for a celebration of the bicentenary of Captain Cook's landing in New Zealand, the

^
The Queen with Emperor Haile Selaisse of Ethiopia admiring the Tissisal Falls, where the Blue Nile begins, during her state visit in 1965.

Queen and Prince Philip made a casual detour down one street, talking to people and shaking their hands. A reporter, Vincent Mulchrone of the *Daily Mail*, used the term 'walkabout' – the word previously used to describe a rite-of-passage wandering by Aborigines in the outback – to record this. So it is that language and Royal protocol evolves.

Some details of the 1966 tour to the Caribbean might help to give a better idea of the nature of the Queen's overseas tours. For the first major overseas trip since the birth of Prince Edward, the Queen and the Duke of Edinburgh made a five-week tour to the Caribbean, in which they travelled from island to island on the Royal Yacht *Britannia*. The tour started on 31 January 1966, with a flight from London to Barbados, delayed after a hoax call saying 'Bomb on board the Queen's VC 10'. They boarded *Britannia*, and sailed to Georgetown, the capital of British Guiana, which was to become independent in just over three months. There had been conflict between those inhabitants of African descent and those of Indian descent. The Queen addressed the crowds around the Parliament building, encouraging them to look forward to a shared future. The visit then continued with an afternoon at Durban Park racecourse, receptions, a children's rally and a visit to the wonderfully-named rural settlement of La Bonne Intention.

Britannia then sailed to Port of Spain, the capital of Trinidad and Tobago, independent since 1962, with the Queen as Head of State. She presided over the official opening of Parliament, outlining what 'My Government of Trinidad and Tobago' were planning. The visit ended with a rally in the Queen's Park Oval, with '1,400 schoolchildren taking part and 24,000 looking on, and what the display lacked in precision, partly because the ground was wet, was more than made up for in colour', as *The Times* reported. Then there were visits to the islands of Tobago, Grenada and St Vincent.

The next port of call was Bridgetown, Barbados, then a colony but which was to become an independent country before the end of the year. The Queen took the salute as the Barbados Regiment marched close to the Bridgetown statue of Lord Nelson – erected in 1813, long before the equivalent in London. The tour continued with visits to a succession of small islands – St Lucia, Dominica, Montserrat, Antigua, St Kitts, Nevis, the British Virgin Islands, and the Turks and Caicos Islands. All were then colonies, but only the British Virgin Islands and the Turks and Caicos Islands now remain as British Overseas Territories. The Duke caused a little stir in Dominica in expressing his forthright views; when visiting a hospital the matron had complained about mosquitoes to which the Duke responded, 'You have mosquitoes – we have the press.'

The Bahamas were next. They had been internally self-governing since 1964 and the opposition leader, Lynden Pindling, used the occasion to petition against the government's corruption – a year later he was premier and became one of the Queen's longest serving ministers, holding office until 1992. The tour ended on the island of Jamaica. Independent since 1962, the Queen, as Queen of Jamaica, opened Parliament, outlining the plans of 'My Government in Jamaica'. *Britannia* sailed to Montego Bay for the last day of the tour and in the evening the Royal party flew back to Britain.

^
The Queen and the Duke of Edinburgh being welcomed in Barbados on their Caribbean tour of 1966.

The Third Decade
1972–1981

Celebrating the wedding of the Prince of Wales to Lady Diana Spencer on the balcony at Buckingham Palace in July 1981.

The Third Decade 1972–1981

The Queen's third decade on the throne saw not only joyful celebrations of her silver wedding but also of her Silver Jubilee and the Royal spectacular that was the wedding of the Prince of Wales and Lady Diana Spencer in 1981. A few cracks were appearing in the 'family on the throne', notably the divorce of Princess Margaret, but overall the Royal family seemed more robust than the nation itself – the three-day week, the 'winter of discontent' and the resounding victory of Mrs Thatcher in the 1979 general election all being products of what appeared to be a divided society.

^
The Queen and the Duke of Edinburgh at the State Opening of Parliament in May 1979 after the general election that brought the Conservatives, under Margaret Thatcher, to power.

The Royal Family

For the Royal family the decade started with a poignant reminder of the past, for on 28 May 1972, the Duke of Windsor died at his home in Paris. The Queen had visited him ten days earlier while she was on a state visit to France, by which time he was already very weak. After his death his body was brought back to Britain to lie in state in St George's Chapel for two days, followed by a private funeral and burial at the Royal Burial Ground at Frogmore within Windsor Great Park. The Duchess was invited to stay at Buckingham Palace, more out of duty rather than compassion. She continued living in Paris until her death in 1986, and was then buried alongside her husband.

Later that year, there was much to celebrate as the Queen and Duke of Edinburgh reached their silver wedding anniversary. There was a thanksgiving service, taken by the Archbishop of Canterbury, at Westminster Abbey to which, in a nod towards public accessibility, 100 couples who had been married on the same day were invited. There followed a celebration lunch at the Guildhall in the City of London. In response to a toast by the Lord Mayor, the Queen said 'I think everyone will really concede on this, of all days, I should begin my speech with "My husband and I".' Afterwards the Queen and the Duke of Edinburgh undertook a walkabout, by then an almost accepted part of Royal occasions since its first appearance in 1970 in New Zealand. *The Times*, in its leader extolled 'that the Queen, the Duke and their children have set a standard of family life and family happiness that everyone must respect and many envy. One can best see what it means to people and to society as a whole if one imagines the opposite for a moment', an unknowing comment on what would happen in the years ahead.

Princess Anne spent much time in training and competing in three-day eventing and it was in this circle that she met Captain

Mark Phillips. May 1973 saw the announcement of their engagement, and their wedding took place at Westminster Abbey on 14 November. The day was declared a public holiday and the celebrations followed a traditional pattern, complete with the appearance of the happy couple on the balcony at Buckingham Palace. Reflecting a different approach from previous generations, Mark Phillips did not accept any title on marrying Princess Anne, and their children (Peter, the Queen's first grandchild, born in 1977 and Zara, born in 1981) have no titles either.

While attention was increasingly turning to the younger generation, it was announced in 1976 that Princess Margaret and Lord Snowdon were separating, divorcing two years later. The publication in February 1976 of photographs of Princess Margaret and her friend Roddy Llewellyn on the island of Mustique, had hastened the separation, but the knowledge that all was not well encouraged newspapers to look harder for unflattering Royal stories (soon to become the life-blood of the tabloid press).

^
The Queen, with her first grandchild, Peter Phillips, and Princess Anne after his christening.

The security of the Royal family became a matter of increasing concern, particularly as the IRA campaign spilled over from Northern Ireland into mainland Britain. The potential exposure of members of the Royal family was highlighted on the night of 20 March 1974 when there was an attempted kidnapping of Princess Anne and Mark Phillips as their car drove down The Mall, in central London. Their car was forced to stop and shots were fired, wounding the chauffeur, their personal detective, a policeman and a journalist who happened to be in a taxi nearby. The attacker, who was arrested, had intended to hold the Royal couple for a £3 million ransom, and while there was relief that the attack had not been undertaken by more ruthless operators, the security implications caused much concern. The Queen was also exposed to danger at Trooping the Colour in 1981 when a teenager fired six blanks from a pistol aimed at her. With calm efficiency the Queen controlled her horse, which was more frightened, she maintained, by members of the Household Cavalry coming towards her than by the shots.

The Queen at Trooping the Colour in 1981, moments after six blank shots were fired at her.

However, the family was not immune from dedicated terrorists. On 27 August 1979 Lord Mountbatten, the Duke of Edinburgh's uncle, was on his fishing boat at Mullaghmore near Sligo in the Republic of Ireland with a family party when it was blown up by a bomb planted by the IRA. Lord Mountbatten and three others were killed and everyone else in the party seriously injured. The shock to the family was immense, for 'Dickie' was a father figure to them. The national revulsion that the IRA could undertake such an outrage was reinforced by further attacks later that day at Warrenpoint, when eighteen British soldiers were killed. Lord Mountbatten was given a solemn state funeral on 5 September at Westminster Abbey and was later buried at Romsey Abbey in Hampshire, close to his home of Broadlands.

This decade ended with perhaps the grandest of all recent Royal events, the wedding of the Prince of Wales and Lady Diana Spencer in 1981. In the preceding years many suitable partners had been suggested for Charles, though his wish to marry Camilla Shand was thwarted by her marriage to Andrew Parker Bowles in 1973, while he was away on duty with the Royal Navy. In

^
The funeral of Lord Mountbatten at Westminster Abbey in 1979.

summer 1980, however, he met Lady Diana Spencer. Diana was born in 1961 at Park House (on the Sandringham estate), which her parents, the Viscount and Viscountess Althorp, rented from the Queen and which remained Diana's home until 1975. Her father had been equerry to George VI and the Queen between 1948 and 1952, and the family were familiar with the ways of the Royal household, indeed the Queen is godmother to Diana's younger brother Charles, and Diana's sister, Jane, is married to Robert Fellowes, who was then assistant private secretary to the Queen. Diana's parents separated in 1967 and divorced in 1969. In 1975 her father inherited the title Earl Spencer and the family moved to Althorp in Northamptonshire. The following year she gained a new step-mother, the Countess of Dartmouth, the daughter of the romantic novelist Barbara Cartland. Diana did not have a distinguished school career and moved to London in 1978 where she undertook minor jobs and shared a flat with friends.

The relationship between Charles and Diana blossomed after the Queen invited her to stay at Balmoral in the autumn of 1980. By November the story had been picked up by the press and their staking out of Diana's flat in London began an undignified intrusion into her private life. Very quickly this unknown nineteen-year-old was the centre of media attention and her image was known around the world. She certainly suffered from the pressure of this attention. What was less certain was the strength of the personal relationship between Charles and Diana, perhaps best summarized in the interview given after the formal announcement of the engagement on 24 February 1981, when they were asked whether they were in love to which Diana replied, 'Of course' and Charles added, 'Whatever "in love" means'. The wedding was set for 29 July 1981.

Unusually for a Royal wedding it was decided to hold the service at St Paul's Cathedral, which could accommodate a larger congregation than the more usual Westminster Abbey – and which also allowed for a longer processional route from the Cathedral back to Buckingham Palace. The build-up to what was expected to be a 'fairy-tale' wedding was enormous. A public holiday was declared and estimates suggest that the ceremony was watched on television by over 750 million people around the world, with a further 250 million listening on radio. Estimates for the number of people lining the streets of London vary from 600,000 to two million.

The focus of much attention was the wedding dress designed by Elizabeth and David Emanuel, a romantic creation of ivory taffeta and lace with a dramatic twenty-five foot train that flowed down the steps of St Paul's as Diana began walking into the Cathedral on the arm of her father, the Earl Spencer. The service was taken by the Archbishop of Canterbury and was attended by 3,500 guests, including representatives of eight of the nine monarchies of Europe – there was no member of the Spanish Royal family present because part of the honeymoon involved a visit to Gibraltar to embark on *Britannia*. The wedding register signed, the couple processed out of the Cathedral and down the steps to an open landau to take them through the streets of London back to Buckingham Palace. When they appeared on the balcony, they bowed to public demand, and sealed the occasion with a wedding kiss. It was the start of a new chapter in the Royal family, and the script turned out to be rather different from the expectations on that happy day. The leader in *The Times* the next day now reads so innocently: 'The national response to the Royal marriage is itself a source of hope. It is no surprise that enjoyment, gaiety and feelings of loyalty should predominate. The people's affection for the Queen and her family and their recognition of the crown as the principle of unity in national life are plain enough.'

1. Charles and Diana after their engagement was announced on 24 February 1981; 2. Charles and Diana during their engagement, with the Queen; 3. The wedding service at St Paul's Cathedral in July 1981; 4. The Prince and Princess of Wales wave to the crowds on their way from St Paul's to Buckingham Palace; 5. The wedding kiss on the balcony of Buckingham Palace.

The Queen in Britain

On 1 January 1973, Britain became a member of the European Economic Community after many attempts, over the years, to become more integrated into Europe. This changed the focus of government foreign policy from the Commonwealth to Europe, and fuelled much political debate for the years to come. The administration of Edward Heath faced continuing battles within the country, and in one attempted show of strength with the mining unions he called a general election for the end of February 1974. Not unusually for the man, he showed no interest in the constitutional role of the monarch in this matter and overlooked the fact that the Queen was in the Cook Islands in the Pacific when the election was called, and was opening the Australian Parliament the day before polling day in Britain. After that, she had to abandon her tour and thirty hours later was back at Buckingham Palace so that she could ask the victor in the general election to form a government. For a few days following the inconclusive result of the election, Heath tried and failed to form an administration; then, no doubt with some relief, the Queen summoned Harold Wilson to the Palace to form an administration in the knowledge that audiences would once again become more than just a duty.

Wilson had indicated to the Queen well in advance of his sixtieth birthday that he intended to resign and though the country was surprised when he announced his intention to resign on 16 March 1976, the Queen was expecting it. The Labour Party quickly chose a successor in Jim Callaghan, another Labour politician with respect for the institution of monarchy. His period of leadership was beset with economic and industrial relations problems and Labour was convincingly defeated in the 1979 general election, bringing in the Conservatives with Margaret Thatcher as the new prime minister. This heralded a period of more rigid and less personal relations between the Queen and the Prime Minister.

Before this political change, however, came the Queen's Silver Jubilee in 1977. The celebrations, as with the Diamond Jubilee, were focused around the coronation weekend at the start of June. Ahead of that weekend, the Queen started to make extended tours around Britain in her wish to meet more people, her first of six tours starting in Glasgow on 17 May. The main celebration started with the lighting of beacons across the land, each being lit when the preceding beacon was seen, replicating the warning used as the Spanish Armada approached in 1588. The first beacon, in Windsor Great Park, was lit by the Queen at ten minutes past ten, her arrival having been delayed by crowds in Windsor. Soon neighbouring beacons were lit and about an hour later the last, on Shetland, was alight.

^
The Queen on a walkabout in north London during the Silver Jubilee celebrations in 1977.

The following day started with a Royal procession from Buckingham Palace to St Paul's Cathedral for a service of thanksgiving, with many people lining the route, hoping for a sight of the Gold State Coach in which the Queen and Duke of Edinburgh were travelling. The Queen and Duke of Edinburgh then walked from St Paul's to the Guildhall, meeting people as they went. At the Guildhall, the Lord Mayor hosted a lunch and then the Royal party returned to Buckingham Palace. The Mall filled with people waiting to see the Queen's balcony appearances. All around the country there were thousands of street parties to celebrate the Jubilee, and the celebrations touched a loyal nerve in many communities. On 9 June, a damp day, the Queen progressed by boat from Greenwich to Lambeth, stopping along the way in Deptford, Bermondsey and St Katharine Docks, where she was met by a cacophony of hooters and claxons from the assembled boats, followed by lunch on *Britannia*, moored by Tower Bridge, and tea with the Archbishop of Canterbury at Lambeth Palace. In the evening, from a position at County Hall, she reviewed a pageant of 140 vessels that sailed from Vauxhall down to Greenwich, before watching a spectacular firework display over the Thames.

^
The Gold State Coach carrying the Queen and Duke of Edinburgh from Buckingham Palace during the Silver Jubilee celebrations.

The Queen around the World

The decade saw the Queen travel widely around the world both as Britain's Head of State and as Head of the Commonwealth, now a much larger collection of nations following the decade of independence in the 1960s. The year 1972, for example, saw an extended Far Eastern tour visiting Thailand, Singapore, Malaysia, Brunei, the Maldives, the Seychelles, Mauritius and Kenya, a state visit to France, and a state visit to Yugoslavia, the first visit by a monarch to a communist country. The Royal party was greeted by Marshall Tito on its arrival and by large crowds in Belgrade and Zagreb – and there was also a visit to a Lipizzaner stud farm in Djakovo.

In 1973 the Queen visited Australia and on 20 October opened one of the world's most iconic buildings, the Sydney Opera House – completed after a long and tortuous design and construction process that had started in 1957. Two years after this visit, the Queen, through her representative in Australia, the Governor-General, Sir John Kerr, became embroiled in a constitutional crisis. The Governor-General, acting in the name of the Head of State, sacked the Labour prime minister Gough Whitlam when he was unable to get his budget bill passed in the House of Representatives. Kerr then appointed Whitlam's Conservative opponent, Malcolm Fraser, as Prime Minister. Although Kerr did keep the Palace informed of the crisis as it progressed, he did not give the Palace news of the sacking of Whitlam until after the event. When the House of Representatives then defeated Fraser in a vote of no confidence, Kerr refused to reinstate Whitlam and instead ordered that both houses of Parliament be dissolved and elections held. There was much debate that Kerr had acted beyond his authority. It certainly fuelled demands within Australia for a new republican constitution with no formal role for the Queen though, when this idea was later put to a referendum in 1999, it was defeated.

In 1976 the Queen travelled to the USA to join the celebrations of the Bicentenary of the Declaration of Independence. The unreality of the occasion was not lost on the Queen – in her Christmas message that year she said 'Two hundred years ago the representatives of the thirteen British Colonies in North America signed the Declaration of Independence in Philadelphia. This year we went to America to join in their Bicentennial celebrations. Who would have thought 200 years ago that a descendent of King George III could have taken part in these celebrations?' From these celebrations, the Queen moved on to Montreal, where she officially declared open the 1976 Olympic Games and was able to see Princess Anne compete in the equestrian events, unfortunately not successfully.

The year 1979 started with the Queen travelling extensively in the Middle East. February and March saw trips to Kuwait, Bahrain, Saudi Arabia, Qatar, the United Arab Emirates and Oman. These visits were all uncontroversial, something which could not be said of her tour to Africa, later in the year.

Her trip to Tanzania, Malawi, Botswana and Zambia came at a difficult time in Britain's relations with the Commonwealth over the continuing failure to resolve the situation in Rhodesia. Mrs Thatcher was intransigent over the prevailing view of the Commonwealth – that negotiations with the opponents of the Smith regime in Rhodesia needed to be undertaken. This topic was to be discussed at the Commonwealth Heads of State Conference to be held in Lusaka in Zambia, which the Queen was to attend. Mrs Thatcher applied some pressure for the whole tour to be cancelled, notionally on the grounds of the Queen's safety, but the Palace resisted. The Queen certainly helped calm the atmosphere and so helped pave the way for a negotiated settlement, not least as a result of the strong personal bonds she had built up with the leaders of the African Commonwealth countries.

1. Sydney Opera House on the day of its opening by the Queen during her tour of Australia in 1973; 2. The Queen dances with President Gerald Ford at a White House State Dinner during the Queen's US Bicentennial visit, Washington DC, July 1976; 3. Just another spectator, as she watches Princess Anne competing in the three-day eventing at the Montreal Olympics in 1976; 4. The Queen greets guests at a banquet she gave in Oman in 1979, during an extensive tour around the Gulf States.

1

2
4

3

The Fourth Decade 1982-1991

The Queen with the Queen Mother, Princess Diana and Prince Charles at the Braemar Games during their annual holiday in Scotland, September 1982.

The Fourth Decade 1982–1991

At the start of this decade everything looked set fair for the monarchy – the sense of magic surrounding the wedding of the Prince and Princess of Wales was fresh in everyone's mind and the Princess of Wales brought both glamour and a contemporary ease in communicating with people. As the decade progressed, the Royal family increasingly came under attack from a press that no longer felt the need for deference – instead laying open Royal marital problems and complaining that the younger Royals were leading lives of leisure at the expense of the taxpayer. While the Queen remained above the turmoil in her family, even she could not escape attack when the tax-free income from her private wealth came under scrutiny.

The Royal Family

The Queen turned sixty in 1986 and at a time when many of her subjects might have considered retiring, she showed no inclination to do so. She was able to enjoy the pleasures of her grandchildren but she faced a number of questions about the administration of the institution of the monarchy during the decade. One issue related to the ineffectiveness of Buckingham Palace security, for on the morning of 9 July 1982 she awoke to find a stranger, Michael Fagan, in her bedroom. Her initial call to the police protection in the Palace went unheeded and she talked to Fagan for around ten minutes before help came to detain him. It was, perhaps, an indication that those working in the Palace had become too comfortable in their ways. Later in the decade there was a major review of how the Palace operated and many changes followed – among the questions the Queen asked during this review was, 'Why do I have so many footmen', an example of how traditions continued long past the need for them.

In November 1981 it was announced that the Princess of Wales was expecting a baby and on 21 June 1982, Price William was born, immediately becoming second in line to the throne after his father. Six week later he was christened William Arthur Philip Louis by the Archbishop of Canterbury at Buckingham Palace. Two years later, on 15 September 1984, Prince Harry was born. He was christened Henry Charles Albert David, again by the Archbishop but this time at St George's Chapel at Windsor Castle. Diana became ever more popular, the first Royal for many generations who could really be regarded as fashionable and aware of the impression she made (and, some believe, quite happy to use the press to promote herself if she could see advantage in it). There were strains in the marriage which were beginning to be noticed. The Palace's approach to such stories of 'never admit and never deny', led the press increasingly to say what it pleased, creating a sense of dysfunction about the marriage.

^
Prince William's christening, held at Buckingham Palace on 4 August 1982.

Prince Andrew, who had joined the Royal Navy in 1979, and in which he continued to serve until July 2001, began to see his romantic affairs featuring in the newspapers. In March 1986 his engagement to Sarah Ferguson, the daughter of Prince Charles's polo manager, was announced. The wedding was held at Westminster Abbey on 23 July that year, at which point Prince Andrew took the title of Duke of York. The Duchess had an outgoing and enthusiastic character and was initially regarded as bringing a breath of fresh air into the Palace corridors, though some courtiers were concerned that there was just a bit too much enthusiasm. Their first daughter, Beatrice Elizabeth Mary, was born on 8 August 1988 and their second daughter, Eugenie Victoria Helena, on 23 March 1990.

^
The Duke and Duchess of York after their wedding on 23 July 1986.

Prince Edward, like his brother, had been sent to Gordonstoun, leaving in the summer of 1982, having been head boy for his last term. In September of that year he went to New Zealand to help at Wanganui Collegiate School for two terms. The next autumn he went up to Jesus College, Cambridge, to study history, graduating in 1986. Following Royal tradition he then started a military career with the Royal Marines, renowned for their tough training programme. After four months, the Prince found that he was unsuited to this life and he resigned to work in theatre and television production. One of his early projects was *The Grand Knockout Tournament*, in which competing teams of celebrities, each captained by a member of the Royal family, took part in a ridiculous games show, a situation made worse when Prince Edward walked out of a press conference after the show. While it raised over a million pounds for charity, it damaged the dignity of the Royal family and fuelled debate about the performance of the family and their finances.

^
Prince Edward at Cambridge University.

The Queen's Palaces

The Queen makes use of a number of Royal residences in Britain (two of which, Balmoral and Sandringham, are privately owned by the Queen).

It is Buckingham Palace that defines the Royal presence in London. The house, originally built for the Duke of Buckingham in 1705, was one of the grandest private houses in London. In 1762 George III purchased it from the Duke's family and it became his main London residence. George IV initiated a major expansion, amidst much argument over costs, and his building works were not completed by the time Queen Victoria moved there in 1837. The familiar East Front of the Palace looking onto The Mall, designed by Sir Aston Webb, was added over the existing front in 1913. It sits in 45 acres of garden, part of which was once a mulberry orchard established by James I to encourage a silk industry.

Henry VIII built St James's Palace, which became the central London heart of the monarchy's administration from 1698 until the time of Queen Victoria. It remains a Royal palace today. Clarence House is in its grounds. Kensington Palace was purchased in 1689 by William and Mary, who enlarged it. The Palace was the main Royal residence in central London until George III moved to Buckingham Palace. Kensington Palace from then on provided apartments for members of the Royal family.

William the Conqueror started to build Windsor Castle in the 1070s, and it has been a Royal castle ever since, claiming to be the largest occupied castle in the world. Many monarchs have added buildings. Edward III built St George's Hall for the Knights of the Order of the Garter, and Edward IV built the spectacular late medieval St George's Chapel, where ten monarchs are buried. Its present Gothic appearance was started by George IV. In 1992 there was a serious fire, and many rooms were damaged. They have now all been restored (see page 103).

Positioned at the bottom of the Royal Mile in Edinburgh, the Palace of Holyroodhouse is on the site of an abbey founded by King David I in 1128 (the ruins of which are attached to the Palace). The building of the Palace started around 1500 and the oldest surviving section is the northwest tower. Most of what we see today was built by Charles II, including all the state rooms, and though the work was finished in the 1670s, he never visited it. It is the Queen's official residence in Scotland.

Sandringham, on the north Norfolk coast, was purchased in 1862 by Queen Victoria as a country retreat for her son, the future Edward VII. The house was rebuilt in 1870 to the design of a local Norwich architect. It has long been a favourite Royal country haunt and is frequently the centre of Christmas festivities.

Balmoral was originally purchased by Queen Victoria in 1848. In 1856 the original 15th century castle was replaced by today's building, designed by an Aberdeen architect with some assistance from Prince Albert. Sitting on the south bank of the river Dee with the mountain of Lochnagar looming up over it, it is used as a late summer retreat for the family, its isolation providing a chance for relaxation away from the attention of the press.

Sandringham near King's Lynn, one of the Queen's privately-owned residences.

The State Dining Room in Buckingham Palace, used when international leaders visit and for larger family events, such as the wedding of William and Catherine in 2011.

THE QUEEN IN BRITAIN

The Queen's fourth decade on the throne started with the invasion of the Falkland Islands by Argentina on 2 April 1982 and the resulting campaign to reclaim them. The Queen was involved both as Head of the Armed Forces, in whose name wars are fought 'for Queen and country', and also as a mother, for Prince Andrew was a helicopter pilot on board HMS *Invincible* that set sail from Portsmouth on 5 April to the South Atlantic. This direct involvement brought extra respect to the monarchy and personal support to the Queen. Prince Andrew took part in the fighting that resulted in the retaking of the Falklands and the surrender of the Argentine forces on 14 June. There was great national and personal celebration when the Queen and the Duke of Edinburgh welcomed home HMS *Invincible* and Prince Andrew to Portsmouth on 17 September.

In spite of the Falkland hostilities, the first ever papal visit to Britain still went ahead. Pope John Paul II arrived at Gatwick Airport for a six-day visit on 28 May, kissing the ground as he stepped away from the aircraft. After celebrating mass at Westminster Cathedral, he went to Buckingham Palace for an audience with the Queen, where the Falklands conflict must have been on both their minds.

In early June Ronald Reagan and his wife made a long-planned state visit, with the Reagans staying at Windsor Castle rather than Buckingham Palace, giving the opportunity for the Queen and President to go riding and for a grand state banquet to be held in St George's Hall. The relations between the two Heads of State were warm, and the visit helped bolster American support for Britain in the Falklands War, which came to a successful conclusion within a few days.

1. Prince Andrew and Sub Lt Ian McAllister at Port Stanley on the Falkland Islands shortly after its recapture in 1982; 2. The Queen, the Duke of Edinburgh and Prince Andrew disembarking from HMS Invincible at Portsmouth on its return from the Falklands on 17 September 1982; 3. The Queen and Pope John Paul II, Buckingham Palace, 1986; 4. The Queen riding with Ronald Reagan in the grounds of Windsor Castle; 5. The Queen rides 'Burmese' during Trooping the Colour in 1986, the last time she rode in the ceremony.

1
2
3
4
5

Up until 1987, every year the Queen attended the Trooping the Colour ceremony on horseback, riding sidesaddle from Buckingham Palace to Horse Guards Parade and remaining on her horse throughout the ceremony. In 1987 for the first time she travelled by open carriage and inspected her troops from the carriage rather than on horseback. The ceremony is one of the main annual Royal events in London and is held to celebrate the Queen's 'official' birthday in the middle of June. The original intention of the ceremony was to carry through the ranks (Troop) the regimental flag (Colour) so that all the regiment's troops would recognize it in battle. The ceremony originated in the early 18th century and started to be used to mark the monarch's birthday from 1748. From the reign of Edward VII, the monarch started to attend in person and take the salute. The Queen first took the salute in 1951 when her father was not well enough to attend. She has taken the salute at every Trooping the Colour during her reign (in 1955 the event was cancelled as a result of a national railway strike). The troops in the ceremony come from the Household Division and the Colour of one regiment from the Grenadiers, Coldstream, Scots, Irish or Welsh Guards is trooped each year. Upwards of 1,000 soldiers and 400 bandsmen take part, creating a great spectacle.

Throughout the 1980s Margaret Thatcher dominated the political landscape in Britain, with convincing victories in general elections in 1983 and 1987, and the Palace's role in the government of the country was limited to the speech given at the State Opening of Parliament, the regular audiences with the Prime Minister and other constitutional matters. By 1990 Margaret Thatcher's popularity in her party was declining and, after a challenge to her leadership suggested that she might not win enough support, she indicated that she would resign on 20 November. This time the party had a mechanism for choosing a successor, so the summons for John Major to the Palace on 28

November was a formality reflecting the settled wish of the party. He was to be her prime minister for the next six years.

On 21 December 1988 Pan Am Flight 103 was blown up in the skies above the Scottish market town of Lockerbie, killing all 259 people on board and a further 11 on the ground at Lockerbie, as well as causing much damage in the town. The next day Prince Andrew visited Lockerbie, but his remarks were thought insensitive to the concerns of the town's residents and further questions were asked when no member of the Royal family attended the memorial service held at Lockerbie on 4 January 1989, where the Queen was represented by the Lord Lieutenant of Dumfries. It was felt that at times of national disasters the Royal family needed to be seen to represent the country. Prince Charles then made an extended visit to the town on 24 January and has returned a number of times since, visits which have been much appreciated.

The Queen around the World

In her fourth decade the Queen seemed to travel even more than usual – indeed in the ten years from 1982 to 1991 she made visits to thirty-one Commonwealth countries (Canada was the most visited, with five separate trips) and eight state visits to other

^
The Queen with six of her Prime Ministers, (left to right) James Callaghan, Sir Alec Douglas-Home, Margaret Thatcher, Harold MacMillan, the Queen, Harold Wilson and Edward Heath, celebrating 250 years of 10 Downing Street as the Prime Minister's residence, 11 December 1985.

countries, including the first state visit by a British monarch to China in 1986. The Commonwealth visits included attendance at all five Commonwealth Heads of Government Meetings, where Britain was frequently fairly isolated over the need for sanctions against the apartheid regime in South Africa. This issue ceased to be divisive towards the end of the decade, particularly after the release of Nelson Mandela from prison in 1990.

Her first overseas trip of the decade was to Canada in 1982, for the proclamation of a new constitution. The process of negotiation over this new settlement had begun four years previously. The outcome was that the Queen was to be known as 'Queen of Canada' but that nearly all her previous constitutional responsibilities were placed in the hands of a Canadian-appointed Governor-General. In effect she became a figurehead for Canada in a redefinition of the term 'constitutional monarchy', a much more satisfactory outcome than the republican option that was regularly discussed in Australia.

The Queen was Head of State of the Caribbean island of Grenada, which had been independent since 1973. On 25 October 1983 US Marines invaded the island, called in, it seems, by the Governor-General, to suppress a left-wing coup. However, all involved appeared to overlook the fact that the Queen was Head of State. She was reported to be most displeased that she had not been informed about these heavy-handed actions to restore order and she certainly did not wish other Commonwealth countries to be so easily invaded by foreign troops. Two years later she visited Grenada and addressed the state opening of the Grenada parliament.

The future of Britain's largest remaining colony, Hong Kong, was becoming a matter of growing concern. Hong Kong was a thriving community with one of the world's most active economies, but much of its territory was leased from China, based on an 1898 agreement (which China regarded as unequal) that ended in 1997. In 1984 an agreement was made between Britain and China to return Hong Kong to Chinese rule in 1997 with certain protections for Hong Kong, which would continue to be administered separately from the rest of China. This agreement helped make possible the first visit of a British monarch to China, which occurred in 1986. The trip included an audience with Deng Xiaoping, the power behind the reforms in China following the death of Mao Tsetung, as well as visits to the Great Wall and to the spectacular 'terracotta army', which had recently been discovered near Xi'an and which date from 220 BC.

^
The Queen with President Li of the People's Republic of China, inspect the troops in Tiananmen Square, Beijing, during the state visit of 1986.

The trip was a great success, though overshadowed in much of the British press by coverage of some off-the-cuff comments by the Duke of Edinburgh.

In the years that followed there were various trips linked to particular events – the 350th anniversary of the Barbados Parliament in 1989 and the 150th anniversary of the Waitangi Treaty in New Zealand in 1990, while in 1991, there were two most significant events. In May, after the ending of the first Gulf War, the Queen visited the USA addressing both Houses of Congress, the first British Head of State to do so (although Prime Ministers had already been given this honour, Churchill having addressed Congress a record three times). In the speech she reflected on the special relationship and on the nature of democratic societies: 'Some people believe that power grows from the barrel of a gun. So it can, but history shows that it never grows well nor for very long. Force, in the end, is sterile. We have gone a better way: our societies rest on mutual agreement, on contract and on consensus.'

At the end of the year there was a meeting of the Commonwealth Heads of Government in Zimbabwe, itself an event that would have been inconceivable ten years earlier, but what made this gathering all the more significant was that it was attended by Nelson Mandela, as an observer. In three years' time he would be President of South Africa and would bring his country back into the Commonwealth after an absence of over forty years. The Commonwealth was in good health and in the years ahead, countries that had had no formal link with Britain were applying for membership – in 1995 Mozambique and Cameroon, neither with any traditional British links, became members, and the most recent member is Rwanda, which joined in 2009.

1. The Queen and the Duke of Edinburgh at the Great Wall, near Beijing, China, October 1986; > *2. The Queen examines part of the 'terracotta army', created to guard the mausoleum of the first Qin emperor over 2,000 years ago, near Xi'an, China; 3. The Queen addresses both chambers of the US Congress at the Capitol during her visit to Washington DC, January 1991.*

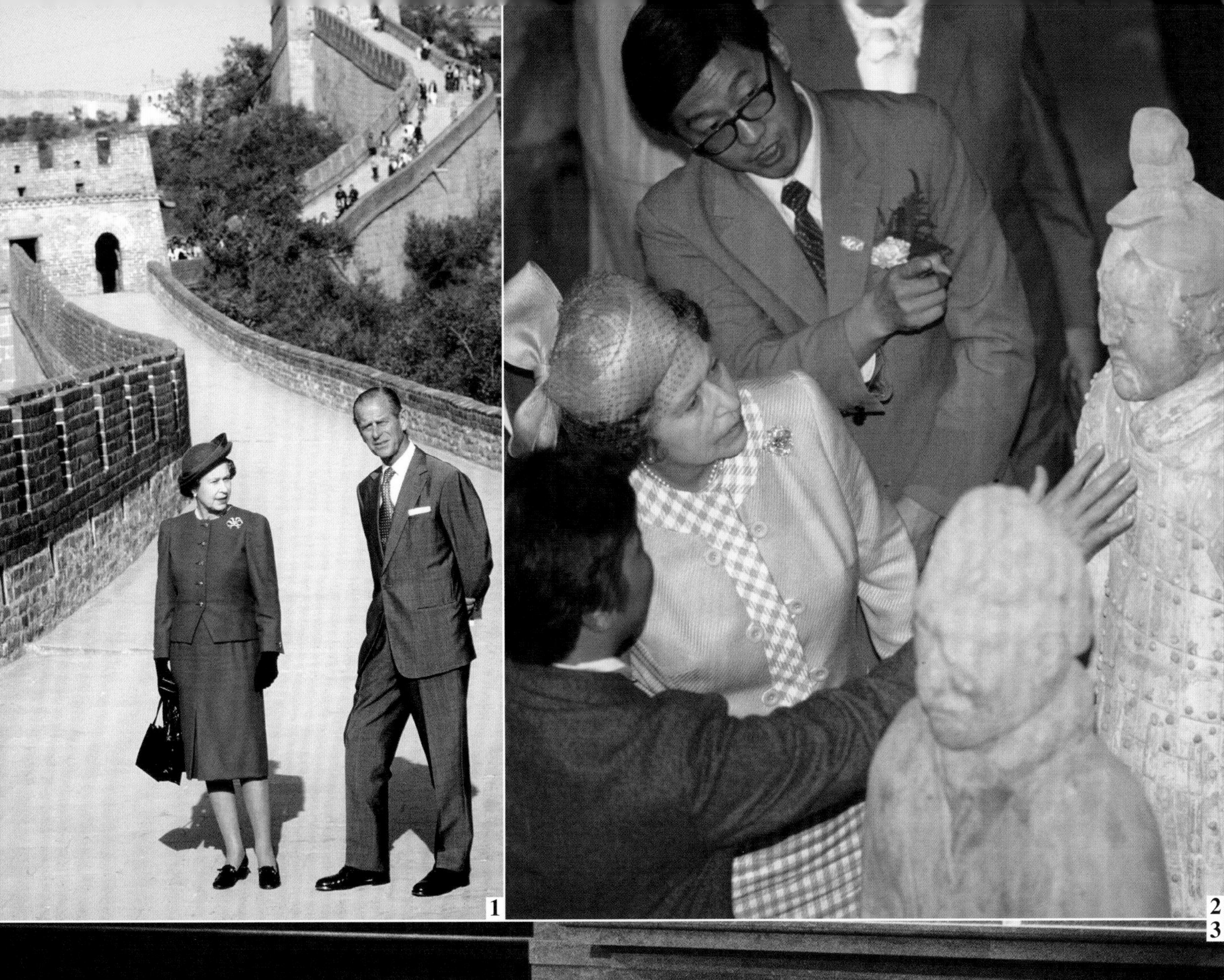

IN GOD WE TRUST

The Fifth Decade
1992–2001

The Queen with President Nelson Mandela of South Africa in The Mall on the way to Buckingham Palace, where he stayed as the Queen's guest, during a state visit to Britain, 9 July 1996.

The Fifth Decade 1992-2001

After forty years on the throne the Queen perhaps hoped that 1992 would bring a bit of calm, but it was not to be. As she said in a speech at the Guildhall on 24 November, '1992 is not a year on which I shall look back with undiluted pleasure. In the words of one of my more sympathetic correspondents, it has turned out to be an *Annus Horribilis*.' The initial Royal response to the death of Diana, Princess of Wales in 1997 looked set to cause further damage to the standing of the Royal family. It managed to pull off a recovery, however, and with judicious changes in style it celebrated the Queen Mother's 100th birthday in 2001 in very British style. It was a transformation indeed.

'Annus Horribilis'

The years leading up to the Queen's fortieth anniversary had seen increased criticism of the monarchy (particularly of its finances and the behaviour of the younger Royals). No major celebration of the anniversary was planned – indeed the Queen had turned down a suggestion that a celebratory fountain be erected in Parliament Square. The Accession Day was marked by a new BBC documentary, *Elizabeth R*, where, once again, the cameras had followed the Queen around for the previous year. Unlike the *Royal Family* documentary, *Elizabeth R* concentrated on the official duties of the Queen and included her own comments on her work and the monarchy. She was shown managing affairs with efficient detachment, with a scene at the Derby generating her most spontaneous moments. She did worry that the younger generation found the regimented side of Royal life hard to live with, words that were only to become too true.

The troubles began in January 1992 when newspapers showed the Duchess of York with a Texan oil millionaire while the

Duke was away at sea and by March, the Duke and Duchess had announced their separation (on the same day as, and distracting the press from, the start of a general election campaign.) 'Fergie's' antics continued throughout the year, providing more embarrassing stories for the press to print.

In April a divorce was granted between the Princess Royal (the Queen had given Princess Anne that title in 1987) and Mark Phillips – they had separated in 1989. At the end of 1992 the Princess Royal married Commander Timothy Laurence, a former equerry to the Queen, at Crathie Church, next to the Balmoral Estate, in a private ceremony. Mark Phillips remarried in 1997, separating again in 2012.

There were more problems in the marriage of the Prince and Princess of Wales. During an Indian tour that the couple made in February, Diana arranged to be photographed sitting alone in an

^
The Duke and Duchess of York, with their children Princess Beatrice and Princess Eugenie, attend the Windsor Horse Show, after the couple's official separation, May 1992.

empty garden in front of the Taj Mahal, that symbol of the love Shah Jahan had for his wife Mumtaz. It was a powerful intimation of a crumbling marriage.

By the time the photograph was taken, Diana already knew that steps she had taken would end the marriage, for in June the serialization started of the book, *Diana, Her True Story*, by Andrew Morton. It provided an account of their unhappy marriage, of her state of mental health and of relations with the wider Royal family, and was written with her encouragement. The publication of the book set the tabloids off in all directions trying to find further stories. More damaging material came to light, especially recordings of telephone conversations between the Princess of Wales and James Gilbey on the one hand and the Prince of Wales and Camilla Parker Bowles on the other. This painfully public exposure of the failed marriage could only lead to the announcement on 9 December that the Prince and Princess were separating. When speaking of the separation in the House

^
The Princess of Wales pictured alone in front of an unnaturally-deserted Taj Mahal during the tour she and the Prince of Wales made to India in February 1992.

of Commons, the Prime Minster, John Major, in the hope of avoiding discussion of potential dynastic difficulties ahead, said that there was no question of a divorce. Diana stayed away from Sandringham that Christmas.

While the Queen was seen as being mostly above the problems in her children's marriages, there was a further issue in which she was directly involved and which became a campaign in a number of newspapers. This was the matter of paying tax on her private income. Discussions had been underway on this topic for some time, albeit making relatively slow progress. In the autumn of 1992 the press latched on to both this topic and the size of the Civil List, the latter prompted by the realization that the last settlement had been too generous in its estimation of inflation. There were comments from both sides of the House of Commons and the issue was clearly not going to go away this time.

However, this debate was interrupted by a devastating fire at Windsor Castle on 20 November. During some restoration work a spotlight in the Private Chapel was pushed against a curtain, starting the fire that quickly spread, gutting St George's Hall and a number of state rooms.

^
The fire at Windsor Castle burning fiercely on the evening of 20 November 1992.

Prince Andrew was at the Castle and helped with the initial rescue plans while the Queen hurried from Buckingham Palace to her beloved castle to see the destruction. Luckily many of the contents of the damaged rooms had already been removed ahead of the restoration work, but moving everything from other parts of the building continued as the firefighters fought to bring the blaze under control. They managed to quell the fire after about fifteen hours and the next morning the true damage could be seen – nine principal rooms and over 100 other rooms had been damaged or destroyed. St George's Hall, the scene of many state banquets, was now a gutted wreck, but no one had lost their life and no great treasurers were lost.

There was, however, a major task of restoration to be undertaken and the government immediately offered to meet the full cost. To the surprise of both the government and the Palace there was a very strong press reaction to this. At a time of economic depression was it right, they argued, that working people should pay for the restoration of a building that was not insured and was used by a very wealthy family? It was soon agreed that the Queen would pay for the restoration, mostly using funds to be generated from opening Buckingham Palace to visitors while the Queen was away at Balmoral in the late summer, a move that turned out to be very commercially successful. The restoration work required many skilled craftsmen and the sourcing of appropriate materials (especially the timbers used to roof St George's Hall). The Queen and the Duke of Edinburgh were able to celebrate their golden wedding anniversary in St George's Hall on 14 November 1997, just under five years after the fire.

The fire had brought further unexpected pressure on the state of the Royal finances and, less than a week after the fire, an announcement was made of reforms that included the agreement by the Queen and the Prince of Wales to pay tax on their private

1. More than 100 rooms were damaged by the fire, the true extent of which can be seen on this aerial view of the Castle taken three days later; 2. The Queen assesses the damage with a firefighter; 3. St George's Hall devastated by the fire in 1992; 4. St George's Hall restored to its former glory, five years after the fire, November 1997.

1
2
3
4

income, and that they would cover the Civil List payments to five members of the Royal family (leaving the state funding just the Queen, the Prince of Wales and the Queen Mother). In all the post-fire debate these major planned changes received less favourable comment than they might have – for they looked as if they were rushed out rather than being the result of long discussions.

In her *Annus Horribilis* speech at the Guildhall, made just four days after the fire, the Queen accepted criticism but just hoped that in future it would not be so harshly done:

No institution – City, Monarchy, whatever – should expect to be free from the scrutiny of those who give it their loyalty and support, not to mention those who don't. But we are all part of the same fabric of our national society and that scrutiny, by one part or another, can be just as effective if it is made with a touch of gentleness, good humour and understanding.

There was some respite to the criticism as the Duke and Duchess of York and Prince and Princess of Wales adjusted to living separated lives. However, Prince Charles arranged with Jonathan Dimbleby to produce an authorized biography to tell his side of the story of the marriage, and combined this with a television interview in autumn 1995 in which he admitted to adultery. Diana returned to the fray the following year by giving an interview to the BBC progamme *Panorama* in November, an interview arranged without the knowledge of the Palace. It was broadcast on 20 November to a massive audience and within it Diana gave her account of the marriage, commenting when asked about Camilla Parker Bowles that, 'There were three of us in this marriage, so it was a bit crowded', and then admitting to her own adultery and her hope that people would remember her as 'the queen of people's hearts'. The Queen's response was swift, writing to both Charles and Diana instructing them to arrange a divorce as soon as possible. The divorce was finalized in August 1996, with a generous settlement for Diana, who would now be known as Diana, Princess of Wales, but no longer with the right to call herself 'Her Royal Highness'. A few months previously, in April, a divorce was also granted to the Duke and Duchess of York.

THE QUEEN AT WORK

There was more to these years than the difficulties within the Royal family. In May 1994, after years of construction, the Queen and President Mitterrand opened the Channel Tunnel. The Queen travelled by train from London to Calais while the French President arrived from Paris. They jointly cut the red, white and blue ribbon. A little later in the day they travelled to Folkestone in the Queen's royal car using the shuttle and performed a similar ceremony at Folkestone. The Queen returned to France with the Duke of Edinburgh on board *Britannia* in June for the fiftieth anniversary of the D-Day landings in Normandy. *Britannia* left Portsmouth for the Normandy coast accompanied by 2,000 ships ranging from the aircraft carrier USS *George Washington* and the *QE2* to small motor boats. The Queen and the Duke attended ceremonies at Bayeux and Arromanches. Later in 1994 the Queen made the first visit to Russia by a British monarch since before the Russian Revolution of 1917.

On 10 May 1994 Nelson Mandela was elected president of South Africa, which then also the returned to the Commonwealth, paving the way for the Queen's visit to South Africa in March 1995, her first visit since 1947. She was enthusiastic to visit the country again and was warmly greeted by many crowds – 'Thank You For Coming Back' proclaimed one banner. She arrived in Cape Town on *Britannia* and was met by President Mandela at the quayside. During her visit she awarded Nelson Mandela the Order of Merit, her personal award, and addressed the South African Parliament, warmly telling them, 'You have become one nation, whose spirit of reconciliation is a shining example to the world.' The following year Mr Mandela would make a trip in the opposite direction, coming to Britain on a state visit of his own, staying with the Queen in Buckingham Palace.

^
The Queen is greeted by South African President Nelson Mandela, as she arrives in Cape Town on Britannia, 20 March 1995.

1996 was also the year that saw the tragic killing of 16 primary school children and their teacher at Dunblane Primary School in Scotland. The event deeply shocked the nation and this time the Palace recognized the monarch's role – four days after the shooting, a memorial service was held on Mothering Sunday in Dunblane Cathedral, which the Queen and the Princess Royal attended. Afterwards the Queen talked to some of the bereaved relatives and visited the injured children and teachers who were still in hospital. The Queen was indeed acting as the representative of her people in supporting the shocked people of Dunblane.

A Year of Sadness and Joy

The year 1997 was to become the most difficult year yet for the monarch, though it did not start that way. The Queen launched the official Royal website in March, a recognition by the Palace that there were new ways of communicating information about the monarchy – and they were rewarded with over 100 million visitors during its first year. The country changed too, for in the general election in May, Labour were returned with an overwhelming majority. On 2 May the Queen summoned Tony Blair to the

^
The Queen and the Princess Royal arrive to lay a wreath at Dunblane Primary School on the day they came to the memorial service for those who were killed.

Palace and asked him to form a government, the Queen noting that he was her first prime minister to have been born during her reign. Her courtiers would certainly have noticed that he was also the first prime minister to have been to a public school since Sir Alec Douglas-Home in 1963.

Two months later saw the effective end of a meaningful empire as Hong Kong was returned to China. Prince Charles attended the handover in Hong Kong and he and the last governor of Hong Kong, Chris Patten, and his family, sailed out of Hong Kong harbour on *Britannia*. It was the last and very symbolic role for *Britannia* that had served the Royal family so well. It was decommissioned at the end of the year, having been deemed by the previous government as too expensive to bring up to the standards of modern maritime regulations. Discussions about a replacement had been underway but the new government felt that it was an expenditure that the country could not afford. It was an emotional moment for the family when it was decommissioned, after which it became a popular tourist attraction at Leith docks, by Edinburgh. During its active life, *Britannia* travelled over a million nautical miles and had been used for official entertaining all over the world as well as for Royal honeymoons and Royal cruises around the islands of the west of Scotland.

The Royal Yacht Britannia in Hong Kong harbour on its last official duty. The Prince of Wales and the Governor of Hong Kong boarded her after the colony had been returned to China on 1 July 1997.

The Queen is clearly moved at the decommissioning ceremony of the Royal Yacht Britannia, Portsmouth, 1 December 1997.

While in an ordinary year these events would be significant, in 1997 they were completely eclipsed by the news that, in the early hours of 31 August, Diana, Princess of Wales was killed in a car crash in the centre of Paris along with her companion Dodi Al Fayed and the car's driver. The driver had been drinking and he lost control of the car whilst trying to get away from the ever-present posse of photographers who pursued Diana wherever she went. The Royal family, including the Princes William and Harry and their father, were staying at Balmoral and the news reached them in the early morning. A very brief statement was issued ('The Queen and the Prince of Wales are deeply shocked and distressed by this terrible news') and the family went to church as normal – indeed there was no mention of Diana's death or prayers for those bereaved in the service. The Prime Minister contacted Balmoral and it was clear that the Queen would say nothing more than the statement and regarded the matter as a private one. She would not speak to the nation but Mr Blair could. Beyond the isolated world of Balmoral, reaction to the death was building, initially focused as anger with the tabloid press. Tony Blair made an impromptu address from his constituency, convincingly done and capturing a mood by describing Diana as 'the people's princess'. As the next few days progressed, there was an extraordinary outpouring of public grief, with carpets of floral tributes left at Buckingham Palace and Kensington Palace and immense queues to sign books of condolence. There was a mood that the Royal family should show some public signs of their private grief, and symbolism, such as the lack of any flag on Buckingham Palace, assumed great significance. It was agreed that there would be a form of ceremonial funeral at Westminster Abbey and that it would be on Saturday 6 September.

The criticism of the Royal family continued to grow and on the Friday afternoon the Queen flew down to London. When her car approached Buckingham Palace, it stopped and the Queen got

1
2
3
4
5
6

out and started to look at some of the tributes. As the crowd began to applaud it seemed the tide was beginning to turn back towards the Queen. She then gave a brief live address to the nation on the six o'clock news, which again was well received. The funeral the next day was watched by an enormous worldwide audience who witnessed Diana's brother, now the Earl Spencer, launch into a withering attack on the press and on the Royal family.

The Queen had responded to the public mood just in time but the institution was shaken by the power of public criticism. Reforms began to be made in the approach to the types of public visits made by the Queen and in reducing official protocol. A number of her visits started to be linked to particular themes – such as banking or the theatre – during which she would make a number of related visits to a variety of different organizations, increasing the variety of people and places she saw.

However, there was only a quiet celebration of the Queen and Duke of Edinburgh's golden wedding in November of that year – it was the first time since George III in 1811 that a monarch had celebrated a golden wedding. There was a service of thanksgiving at Westminster Abbey followed by a celebration lunch hosted by the Prime Minister. In an extravagant speech he concluded, 'You are our Queen. We respect and cherish you. You are, simply, the best of British.'

Prince Edward, who had been making a quiet career in television production and who had started to pick up more Royal duties as his parents grew older, became engaged in January 1999 to Sophie Rhys-Jones, a public relations consultant. The wedding was on 19 June 1999 and, reflecting changed times, was held at

< 1. Diana Princess of Wales meets children at a school in Neasden, London, June 1997; 2. After her death on 31 August 1997, a huge popular response saw the gardens of Kensington Palace covered by floral tributes; 3. The Prince of Wales, Prince William and Prince Harry look at the tributes at Kensington Palace; 4. The Queen receives a flower by a well-wisher after she had paid her respects to Diana, whose coffin was lying in the Chapel Royal at St James's Palace; 5. Prince Philip, Prince William, the Earl Spencer (Diana's brother), Prince Harry, and Prince Charles follow the funeral cortege to Westminster Abbey, on the day of the funeral, 6 September; 6. The Union flag flies at half mast over Buckingham Palace on the day of the funeral of Diana, Princess of Wales. It was the first time that the flag has flown at half mast over the Palace.

Windsor and on a smaller scale than his brothers' weddings. On marriage they became the Earl and Countess of Wessex.

This year also saw a change in the constitutional arrangements for Scotland and Wales. Following positive referendums in 1997 a Scottish Parliament and a Welsh Assembly were established with powers devolved from Westminster. The Queen attended the opening of the initial session of both these new institutions in 1999.

The Earl and Countess of Wessex on their wedding day.

The Queen in Edinburgh for the opening of the Scottish Parliament.

These were occasions of notable warmth unlike the opening of the much-derided Millennium Dome at the very start of the new millennium. The expression seen on the Queen's face reflected most people's view of the folly of the Millennium Dome.

Much more to public taste was the enthusiastic celebration of the Queen Mother's 100th birthday in 2000, with over 40,000 gathering in The Mall to see her travel by carriage from Clarence House to Buckingham Palace for a family celebration. A few days previously there had been a very English pageant to celebrate her birthday which included marching bands carnival floats, choirs, Aberdeen Angus bulls, Corgi dogs and a parade with representatives of around 320 charities that she had been involved in. It took the oldest member of the family to help build the restoration of faith in the monarchy.

^ *New Year's Eve at the Millennium Dome on 31 December 1999, with Prime Minister Tony Blair.*

^ *The Queen Mother with her two daughters at Buckingham Palace on her 100th birthday.*

The Sixth Decade 2002–2011

Queen Elizabeth ll and Prince Philip, Duke of Edinburgh, revisit Broadlands to mark their diamond wedding anniversary, 20 November 2007. The couple spent their wedding night at Broadlands in Hampshire, the former home of Prince Philip's uncle, Earl Mountbatten, in November 1947.

The Sixth Decade 2002-2011

The new millennium brought national respect back to the Royal family. The Queen's position as the mother and grandmother of the nation was secure once again. Her smile seemed to be everywhere and her undiminished commitment to her role as the years pass by is greatly admired. Her children, with the occasional ruffle here and there, have settled into a more middle-aged existence and attention has moved towards the next generation and their more relaxed approach to their position. The press has been more subdued, a mixture of greater Palace media skills and the impact of the phone-hacking scandal on press behaviour, a scandal that started with the discovery that Royal phones had been hacked in order to obtain stories. The Royal wedding of Prince William and Kate Middleton provided a celebratory prelude to the Diamond Jubilee while the Queen's visit to Ireland showed that she was still prepared to undertake potentially risky visits that less experienced Heads of State would be challenged by.

^
The Queen and Prince of Wales enjoying the tug-of-war at the Braemar Highland Games in 2010.

The Royal Family

Her sixth decade started with great personal loss for the Queen. On 9 February 2002 her younger sister Margaret died, having been in poor health for a number of years. Since her divorce in 1978, Princess Margaret had continued to live a private life at some distance from the Royal family, spending time at her home on the Caribbean island of Mustique. She continued to perform a number of Royal tasks and maintained her patronage of various organizations, particularly in the fields of child protection, nursing, medicine and ballet, but she had a low public profile. Her children were able to pursue independent careers (as a furniture designer and artist respectively) without the press interest that their cousins attracted. In 1998 she suffered a mild stroke and the following year she scalded her feet badly and was thereafter restricted in her walking. She died after a further stroke and there was a private funeral at St George's Chapel at Windsor Castle on 15 February 2002. It was her wish to be cremated and her ashes were placed in the Royal vault.

Princess Margaret, as Colonel-in-Chief of the Queen Alexandra Royal Army Nursing Corps, visiting a military hospital unit in 2000.

The Queen Mother was able attend her daughter's funeral, but this was her last appearance in public. She died peacefully at home at Royal Lodge in Windsor Great Park on the afternoon of 30 March. In his official statement the Prime Minister said of her that 'during her long and extraordinary life, her grace, her sense of duty and her remarkable zest for life made her loved and admired by people of all ages and backgrounds, revered within our borders and beyond.' Before the funeral at Westminster Abbey, her coffin lay in state in Westminster Hall, where around 200,000 people paid their last respects. At one point, her four grandsons, Princes Charles, Andrew and Edward and Viscount Lindley, mounted a vigil around the coffin as the sons of George V had done in 1936. On the day of her funeral, more than a million people lined the streets on the route between Westminster and Windsor, where she was buried alongside her husband in St George's Chapel.

^
The coffin of the Queen Mother lying in state at Westminster Hall. The coffin is draped in the Queen Mother's personal standard.

THE QUEEN

It was a decade of landmarks: 2002 was the Queen's Golden Jubilee (see below), while in 2006 she celebrated her eightieth birthday, in 2011 the Duke of Edinburgh reached his ninetieth

birthday and in between, in 2007, they jointly celebrated their diamond wedding anniversary. The Queen is the first monarch to reach such a landmark. Her actual eightieth birthday was celebrated with her family in Windsor. On her official birthday in June there was a service of thanksgiving at St Paul's Cathedral on 15 June and Trooping the Colour two days later with a special fly-past to mark the occasion. A sense of duty still drives the Queen and the Duke of Edinburgh – although they now do less that they used to, with other members of the family picking up more engagements. They still remain a most active couple as they support each other more in their duties as the Diamond Jubilee approaches. They have been blessed with good health, the Duke recovering quickly from his brief stay in hospital over Christmas 2011, when treatment for chest pains required the fitting of a coronary stent.

^
The Queen with a few of the 20,000 birthday cards she received on her eightieth birthday.

The Queen as a Mother

After the tumult of the previous two decades, greater stability returned to the lives of her children. The Prince of Wales continued to devote time to his many causes from the Prince's Trust to debating ideas of architectural taste. He was also to gain happiness in his personal life – for in 2005 in a civil ceremony at Windsor Guildhall he married Camilla Parker Bowles. The ceremony was followed by a service of prayer and dedication in St George's Chapel, taken by the Archbishop of Canterbury, and a reception at the Castle. Camilla took the title Duchess of Cornwall on marrying the Prince of Wales, clearly distancing herself from the Prince's first wife. It was indicated that she would be known as the Princess Consort when her husband accedes to the throne. Such a settlement is now deemed acceptable, a sign of the way society and the position of marriage has changed since Charles's great uncle chose abdication so that he could marry his previously divorced fiancée. The Duchess has joined the Prince on many of his visits in Britain and overseas and has also undertaken her own visits and has selected various charities to be involved in.

^
The Prince of Wales and the Duchess of Cornwall leaving the service of prayer and dedication at St George's Chapel, at which their marriage was blessed.

Princess Anne, the Princess Royal, maintains a very active Royal life, undertaking over 500 Royal engagements every year. She has been President of the Save the Children Fund since 1970, is actively associated with over 200 charities, and is also on the London Organizing Committee for the London 2012 Olympic Games. Her husband, Tim Laurence, retired from the Royal Navy in 2011, having reached the rank of Vice-Admiral. Prince Andrew, the Duke of York, has not remarried since his divorce from the Duchess of York and they still remain close friends. After leaving the Royal Navy in 2001, he acted as Special Representative for International Trade and Investment, but stood down from this position in July 2011 at a time when some of his business connections were being criticized. He is now undertaking further Royal engagements on behalf of his parents. Prince Edward, the Earl of Wessex, has also become more active in carrying out Royal engagements. He ceased working for his television production company in 2002 while the Countess of Wessex withdrew from her public relations work at the same time. They have two young children, Louise, born in 2003 and James, born in 2007, the Queen's youngest grandchild.

^
Sophie, Countess of Wessex, and her son James Windsor, Viscount Severn, Peter Phillips, Prince Edward, Earl of Wessex, Autumn Phillips, Lady Louise Windsor and Princess Eugenie disembark the Hebridean Princess with other members of the Royal family in Scrabster Harbour in the north of Scotland, 2 August 2010.

The Queen as a Grandmother

The Queen's grandchildren have brought a breath of fresh air into Royal circles, and, by all accounts, have kept the Queen up to date – they have, one imagines, shown their grandmother her recent official presence on YouTube, Facebook and Twitter. Prince William, speaking of his 'granny' in 2012 said how interested she is in all they are doing – 'when we were young it was very easy to take our grandmother for granted. It's only [recently] that I've actually learned to understand and accept the huge deal she is around the world.'

Prince William is second-in-line to the throne. He was educated at Eton, breaking the family link with Gordonstoun. After a gap year, which involved some work on projects in South America and Africa, he went to the University of St Andrews in the autumn of 2001, graduating in 2005. He started by studying history of art but then changed to geography. His time at university was remarkably free from press intrusion, allowing him to build his own group of friends, among whom was Kate Middleton, his future wife. Not long after graduation he entered Sandhurst and gained his commission as an army officer – his graduation parade took place in front of his grandmother and father in December 2006. He became an officer in the Blues and Royals, part of the Household Cavalry. He had expressed a wish to see active service, which led to much debate over whether an heir to the throne should potentially be put at such risk. He continued to gain more military skills and the issue was resolved by William becoming a search and rescue helicopter pilot with the RAF; since early 2010 he has been based at RAF Valley in Anglesey. He has, in addition, undertaken a number of Royal functions and, with his brother, has worked for charitable causes, particularly those which were enthusiasms of his mother. In November 2010

1. Prince William at the controls of a Sea King helicopter during a training exercise out of RAF Valley in Anglesey, North Wales, March 2011; 2. Zara Phillips carries the Olympic flame whilst riding her horse, Toytown, on day 5 of the 70-day Olympic Torch Relay tour of the UK, May 23, 2012; 3. Princess Eugenie attends the Easter Matins service at St George's Chapel, Windsor, 8 April 2012; 4. The Queen smiles at Prince Harry as she inspects soldiers at their passing-out Sovereign's Parade at Sandhurst, 12 April 2006; 5. Peter Phillips with his daughter Savannah at the Lacombe Horse Trials in 2012; 6. Princess Beatrice attends a ball in aid of the Starlight Foundation, October 2011.

1
2
3
4
5
6

his engagement was announced to Kate Middleton, his long-term girlfriend, and preparations began for a major Royal event (see page 133).

Prince Harry followed his brother to Eton, which he left in 2003, and he then took a gap year partly in Australia and partly in Lesotho. When he returned he decided upon a military career and entered Sandhurst in 2005, gaining his commission the following year in April (ahead of his brother). He was commissioned into the Blues and Royals and saw active service in Afghanistan in late 2007 – though was withdrawn when news of his posting leaked out. At the start of 2012 he was in the final stages of training to be an army helicopter pilot. He also has undertaken a number of Royal engagements and as patron of Sentebale, which he established, he raises funds for orphans of AIDS victims in Lesotho. He was his brother's supporter (the Royal equivalent of best man) at his wedding and his easy style with people is reminiscent of his mother.

The profile of the Queen's other grandchildren is lower, though they are not immune from the critical eye of the press. Peter Phillips, the Queen's eldest grandchild, has a full-time career in sports sponsorship. He married Autumn Kelly in 2008 and they have two children, Savannah, born in 2010 and Isla, born in 2012, providing the Queen with her first two great-grandchildren. Zara Phillips followed her mother in her love of, and skill in, three-day eventing, becoming European Champion in 2005 and 2006, and in 2006, like her mother before her, she became the BBC Sports Personality of the Year. In 2011 she married Mike Tindall, an English international rugby player, at the Canongate Kirk in Edinburgh. Princess Beatrice, Prince Andrew's elder daughter, graduated from Goldsmiths, University of London in 2011 while Princess Eugenie started her three-year course at Newcastle University in 2009.

The Queen as Head of State

In 2002 the Queen celebrated her Golden Jubilee. As with the Silver Jubilee and the Diamond Jubilee, the main celebrations were held around the Coronation weekend rather than the time of Accession in February. Indeed in February, though a little while after the Accession Day and her sister's funeral, the Queen was travelling in warmer climes, visiting Jamaica and then flying on to New Zealand and Australia (a visit which included the Commonwealth Heads of Government meeting). Once back home the Queen undertook a very extensive tour of Britain – between May and August she visited over seventy towns and cities. The main focus was on the Jubilee Weekend, with two major concerts taking place in the grounds of Buckingham Palace, including 'the Party at the Palace', apparently watched by 200 million people around the world. What was noticeable was the range of events designed to appeal to a wide variety of people, from street parties, processions and celebratory beacons to military displays and a travelling exhibition of Leonardo drawings from the Royal Collection. Fears that the celebrations would not be enthusiastically supported, which had surfaced at the start of the year, were quickly forgotten and the Queen's position as Head of State was further reinforced. The dark days of the monarchy in the 1990s seemed a long way away.

^
The Queen and Prince Philip in the Gold State Coach during the procession from Buckingham Palace to St Paul's Cathedral on the occasion of the Golden Jubilee.

In 2007 Tony Blair, her prime minister for the last ten years, resigned and she asked Gordon Brown, the approved Labour Party choice, to become the next prime minister. His period in office, and indeed his relationship with the Queen, was not a great success and he was defeated in the 2010 general election.

^
Concorde and the Red Arrows formed part of the Golden Jubilee fly-past. More than a million people crowded into The Mall to watch the spectacle.

The result of the election was not conclusive, however, and the Queen had to wait until it was clear that a coalition government of Conservatives and Liberal Democrats could be formed. Once this was agreed, which took five days, Gordon Brown resigned and the Queen asked David Cameron, the Conservative leader, to form a government and become her youngest prime minister.

Over the years the Queen has met hundreds of thousands of people, some the key figures of the twentieth and twenty-first centuries, others, everyday folk who have perhaps done something special which merits a Royal handshake. Always accommodating and at ease with people, the last decade of her reign has seen the Queen become even more approachable and open to new trends. Often she shows and receives respect from those who seem to have a completely different outlook on life and their own position in the world, but almost every time these meetings end with highly positive feelings on all sides. Here she is meeting Ozzie Osbourne and Kermit the Frog as part of the Party at the Palace in 2002, and below meeting Lady Gaga after the Christmas Royal Variety Performance in Blackpool, December 2009.

THE QUEEN AROUND THE WORLD

As Head of State, the Queen took part in many state visits in her sixth decade – entertaining eighteen heads of state who visited Britain and visiting thirteen countries as Head of State, (including two visits to the USA – and as Head of the Commonwealth visiting a further eleven countries (including two visits to Australia and three to Canada). Invitations for heads of state to visit Britain are given by the government and can sometimes create political tensions, none more so than the visit in 2005 of President Hu Jintao of China. The Queen's visit to China in 1986 was groundbreaking. Since then China had changed in many ways but still it remains a communist dictatorship, and the political gulf between the President and the Queen was enormous, not that the demeanour of the Queen would ever indicate this.

In 2007 the Queen travelled to the USA to celebrate the 400th anniversary of the first successful attempt at British colonization of America at Jamestown, Virginia, named after the Queen's ancestor King James I. She was back again in 2010, a trip which included a visit to the site of 9/11 and her second address to the General Assembly, noting that she was last there in 1957,

^
Chinese President Hu Jintao and his wife Liu Yongqing with Queen Elizabeth ll and Prince Philip, on the evening of the first day of a three-day day state visit to London, 8 November 2005.

and was speaking as 'Queen of sixteen United Nations Member States and as Head of the Commonwealth of 54 countries'. She concluded her speech recalling that 'In my lifetime, the United Nations has moved from being a high-minded aspiration to being a real force for common good. . . . But we are not gathered here to reminisce. In tomorrow's world, we must all work together as hard as ever if we are truly to be United Nations.' The following year President Obama paid a state visit to Britain and was entertained at Buckingham Palace.

Of all her official visits during her sixth decade, perhaps the one that will leave the most lasting effect was the trip to the Republic of Ireland in 2011, the first of a British monarch since Irish independence in 1922. For the Queen there were also personal emotions for it was in Ireland that Lord Mountbatten was assassinated by the IRA, directly linking her with other families

^
The Queen and President Obama outside Buckingham Palace ready to inspect the guard, on a windy day, during his state visit in 2011.

who have suffered from the violence of the conflict in Northern Ireland. There were moments of great symbolism, including dignified respect shown at the Garden of Remembrance to those who gave their lives for Irish freedom, and the visit to Croke Park, home of Gaelic football and hurling and the scene of the 1920 killing of fourteen people by the police.

At a state banquet in Dublin Castle, once the centre of the British administration, the Queen started her speech with a greeting in Irish and then spoke of the troubled history between the two countries:

> *Indeed, so much of this visit reminds us of the complexity of our history, its many layers and traditions, but also the importance of forbearance and conciliation, of being able to bow to the past, but not be bound by it. . . . It is a sad and regrettable reality that through history our islands have experienced more than their fair share of heartache, turbulence and loss. These events have touched us all, many of us personally, and are a painful legacy.*

^
The Queen lays a wreath in the Garden of Remembrance in Dublin, 17 May 2011, the first day of her historic four-day visit to Ireland.

We can never forget those who have died or been injured, and their families. To all those who have suffered as a consequence of our troubled past I extend my sincere thoughts and deep sympathy. With the benefit of historical hindsight we can all see things which we would wish had been done differently or not at all.

She then talked of the hopes for the future, particularly building on the current settlement in Northern Ireland. These really were important words, close to an apology, all the more powerful in coming from a Head of State with no political side. The praise for her speech was widespread and the visit continued in a more relaxed style, including time at the Irish National Stud, near Kildare.

Prime ministers and archbishops may know more of the Queen's personal views from discussions in their confidential audiences, but to everyone else the Queen has mastered the skill of not showing or indicating what she thinks, and very seldom is her guard down. Some may say that she should take the initiative rather than be reactive to events, but she knows that her approach has served her well over sixty years and has mostly kept the monarchy above political debate.

The Royal Wedding

Perhaps, however, there was no better preparation for the Diamond Jubilee year than the wedding of Prince William to Catherine (Kate) Middleton, his girlfriend from his student days in St Andrews. Their engagement was announced on 10 November 2010 and the engagement ring that William gave Kate was his mother's, a reminder of one person who would not be able to join the celebrations. Until Kate met William at St Andrews, she and her family had had no connection with the Royal family or with the aristocratic establishment. Kate's parents have created their own successful business and she would bring a good dose of more normal life into the Royal family. The wedding was fixed for 29 April 2011 at Westminster Abbey and the wedding day was declared a national holiday. The occasion contained a balance of a great Royal occasion, complete with open coach ride from Westminster Abbey to Buckingham Palace and the obligatory kiss on the balcony, with a feeling that this was very much an event celebrating a personal pledge between two people. The service, taken by the Archbishop of Canterbury with a sermon from the Bishop of London, was broadcast to maybe as many as a billion people yet the heart of the service somehow managed to retain a personal feel, summed up in a prayer that the couple wrote for their wedding day: 'God our Father, we thank you for our families; for the love that we share and for the joy of our marriage. In the busyness of each day keep our eyes fixed on what is real and important in life and help us to be generous with our time and love and energy. Strengthened by our union help us to serve and comfort those who suffer. We ask this in the Spirit of Jesus Christ. Amen.'

After their marriage they took the title of Duke and Duchess of Cambridge. It was a day for great family celebration but it also showed how far the perception of the monarchy had moved since the 1990s, and gave a foretaste of national enthusiasm for the Queen's Diamond Jubilee. *The Times*, in its leader on the wedding, caught this sentiment: 'The wedding powerfully demonstrated the value of the monarchy. It provided a moment for the nation to come together, without partisan disagreement, without excuse for political discord. At a moment when so much is hard for Britain, when national morale is low, there was sunshine and laughter and happiness that everyone could join in, and share, if they wanted to.'

1. Prince William and Catherine Middleton announce their engagement, November 2010; 2. Catherine arrives with her father, Michael Middleton, followed by sister of the bride and Maid of Honour, Pippa Middleton, Westminster Abbey, 29 April 2011; 3. The Service begins in front of 1900 guests; 4. The kiss on the Buckingham Palace balcony; 5. The wedding group in the Throne Room at Buckingham Palace. >

1
2
3
4
5

Diamond Jubilee Year

The Queen is cheered by crowds as she arrives at Nine Springs Park in Yeovil, Somerset, 2 May 2012: The Queen and Duke of Edinburgh are on the South West leg of their Diamond Jubilee Tour.

Diamond Jubilee Year

On 6 February 2012, Accession Day, the Queen was 85 years old and the world's oldest reigning monarch. She was Head of State in the UK and 15 other Commonwealth realms, and had reigned through more than five decades of enormous social development and change. In her 60 years on the throne, fashions had come, gone and come again, the Cold War had thawed and 12 prime ministers had formed governments – and her dignity and dedication had made the Royal family more popular than ever. As a young princess, Elizabeth had vowed to serve the Commonwealth, saying:

I declare before you all that my whole life, whether it be long or short, shall be devoted to your service and the service of our great imperial family to which we all belong.

In 2012 the Queen marked the anniversay with an Accession Day message renewing her vow to the nation:

In this special year, I dedicate myself anew to your service.

The anniversary of the Queen's Accession also prompted many messages of respect and devotion from numerous people, most notably Prime Minister David Cameron who said:

Some people characterized the monarchy as simply 'a glittering ornament, a decoration on our national life'. That misunderstands our constitution and it underestimates our Queen. Always dedicated, always resolute and always respected, she is a source of wisdom and continuity. All my life, and for the lives of most people in this country, she has always been there for us. Today, and this year, in the 60th anniversary of her reign, we have the chance to say thank you.

Although Accession Day itself marked a momentous historic milestone, the Queen chose to observe it in the kind of modest, respectful manner that has defined her reign. The Queen travelled from her snowbound Sandringham estate in Norfolk to nearby King's Lynn where, despite the icy temperatures, 150 members of the public stood waiting outside the town hall to see her arrive. She greeted the well-wishers, received some tearfully joyous messages of support, then went to spend time with children at Dersingham Infant and Nursery School. She seemed to enjoy this, her first Diamond Jubilee visit, tremendously. One class had cheekily turned their classroom into a 'royal laundry' after imagining the underwear that a monarch might wear for a school visit. White undergarments dotted the ceiling and dangled from a clothes line.

The school's 130 pupils donned rock and roll-style prom dresses from the 1950s and glitter-spangled suits from the 1970s to present a 15-minute song-filled play about how the world has changed since the Queen acceded to the throne. At one point she was entertained with a rendition of the Time Warp – a particularly apt choice of song. She then returned to Sandringham and spent the afternoon with Prince Philip, perhaps also looking forward to the incredible celebrations that would mark her Diamond Jubilee in the months to come.

One familiar face at King's Lynn was Mary Relph – a royal watcher who has attended hundreds of the Queen's engagements and who was celebrating her own 78th birthday. Mary has followed the Royals for 64 years – and even received a piece of the Duke and Duchess of Cambridge's wedding cake as a thank you for her loyalty.

Beginning with a Bang

Elsewhere around the country, many other events were taking place to mark the start of this jubilee year. On 6 February The King's Troop Royal Horse Artillery were involved in one of the most notable. In full dress uniform and fresh from a parade ground inspection at their barracks in St John's Wood, the immaculate troops were on their way to fire a special 41-gun salute in Hyde Park. Delighted crowds thronged the route as they made their stately progress through the capital's streets. Hundreds more people stamped their feet and tugged their woolly hats tightly over their ears under the trees in the snowy park as the gunners made their preparations. Then came the order to fire and a deafening cannonade rang out into the morning. Each blast was followed by cheers. The celebrations for the Queen's Diamond Jubilee had officially begun.

A Royal Salute is normally of 21 guns, but this is increased to 41 if the salute is fired from a Royal residence or park, while 62 rounds are fired from the Tower of London on Royal anniversaries. HRH Prince Michael of Kent, Master Gunner of the Tower of London, watched from near Tower Bridge as this full salute was also given. The 62 rounds were fired at ten second intervals on three L118 Ceremonial Light Guns, similar to those used in Afghanistan.

^
Soldiers from the King's Troop Royal Horse Artillery fire a 41-gun salute in Hyde Park.

In Scotland, a 21-gun Royal Salute was fired by the 105 Regiment Royal Artillery at Edinburgh Castle at noon. Another was carried out by the Royal Navy at Gosport, Hampshire.

Accession Day started the ball rolling on a spectacular series of national and international events to celebrate the Queen's 60-year reign. Packed with pageantry and glamour, the programme included a tour of the whole country by the Queen and the Duke of Edinburgh, visits by other Royals to the Commonwealth, and culminated in a remarkable jubilee weekend in June. Even after the extended jubilee weekend extravaganza, a series of projects have created a legacy of the Queen's service for the generations to come.

^
Prince Michael of Kent joins soldiers of the Honorable Artillery Company in a 62-gun salute at the Tower of London.

Commonwealth Day service at Westminster Abbey

One of the first big events of the jubilee year was the Commonwealth Day service at Westminster Abbey on 12 March. It was attended by the Queen, the Duke of Edinburgh, the Prince of Wales, the Duchess of Cornwall, the Countess of Wessex, and Prime Minister David Cameron, as well as representatives from Commonwealth countries, many other dignitaries, and 1,000 schoolchildren.

The flags of 53 Commonwealth countries were paraded through the Abbey at the start of the service before the Commonwealth Secretary-General HE Kamalesh Sharma read the Act of Affirmation to the Commonwealth. The Address was given by Dr Jane Goodall DBE, Scientific Director, Mahale-Gombe Wildlife Research Institute, Tanzania. Liz Lochhead read her poem *Connecting Cultures* and there were performances by Rufus Wainwright, Hugh Masekela and the Descarga Dance Company and the Commonwealth Youth Orchestra. Soprano Laura Wright sang a new song *Stronger As One* composed by Robert Hartshorne especially for Commonwealth Day 2012.

The Dean of Westminster, the Very Reverend Dr John Hall, gave some rousing words of thanks:

In the Queen's Diamond Jubilee year, we recall in particular Her Majesty's coronation here on 2nd June 1953. We give thanks for sixty years of faithful service to this Nation, the Realms, and the whole Commonwealth under God.

The Queen also delivered a special Commonwealth Day message:

This year, our Commonwealth focus seeks to explore how we can share and strengthen the bond of Commonwealth citizenship we already enjoy by using our cultural connections to help bring us even closer together, as family and friends across the globe.

Guests and performers at the Commonwealth Day Service, Westminster Abbey, 12 March 2012: >
1. Sophie, Countess of Wessex; 2. John Major (former UK Prime Minister), 3. Camilla, Duchess of Cornwall; 4. Hugh Masekela (South African musicician); 5. Rufus Wainwright (US-Canadian singer).

2
3
5

Royal Maundy Service at York Minster and visit to York

On 5 April the Queen, accompanied by the Duke of Edinburgh and Princess Beatrice of York, attended the Royal Maundy Service at York Minster. During the Maundy service the Queen gave the symbolic alms of 'Maundy money' – small silver coins – to 86 women and 86 men, one for each year of her life. The ceremony derives from an instruction, or *mandatum*, given by Christ at the Last Supper that his followers should love one another. In the Middle Ages, English monarchs washed the feet of beggars in imitation of Jesus, and presented gifts and money to the poor.

For her jubilee year the Queen gave each recipient two purses, one red and one white. The red purse held a £5 coin commemorating the Diamond Jubilee and a 50p coin, both specially minted in 2012. The white purse contained uniquely minted Maundy money in the form of silver one, two, three and four penny pieces totaling 86 pence – the Queen's age this year. The recipients were retired pensioners of all denominations, nominated in recognition of their service to their church and the community in York. To specially mark the Diamond Jubilee, additional recipients were chosen from every diocese and country within the United Kingdom.

Dr John Sentamu, The Archbishop of York, conducted the ceremony.

Princess Beatrice attended the Maundy service with her grandparents, the Queen and the Duke of Edinburgh.

For the Queen, the Royal Maundy service is an important part of her devotional life, and the only occasion on which she visits others to make awards. Usually recipients of honours come to her.

The Queen's face lights up Buckingham Palace

One of the more unusual events of the jubilee celebrations happened on 19 April when Buckingham Palace was lit up by the Queen's smile. The building formed the spectacular backdrop for 32 huge projected images of Her Majesty. These 15m (49ft) high images were made up of 6,400 different children's self-portraits – an incredible 204,800 images in total. Twenty-four projectors were used to cover the entire facade of the Palace with images, including two 15x10m images of the Queen. The luminous landmark was displayed for three consecutive nights as part of the *Face Britain* project, which was organized by The Prince's Foundation for Children & the Arts.

The record-breaking artwork aimed at empowering children to explore their identity creatively, and give the country a unique snapshot of our future generation. Self-portraits by well-known artists, the Prince of Wales and celebrities including Adele, Jamie Oliver and Sir Cliff Richard were also auctioned for the charity.

^
A mosaic of more than 200,000 separate images are projected onto the front of Buckingham Palace, to make up resemblances of the Queen's face and other artworks and self-portraits.

Diamond Jubilee Pageant at Windsor Castle

From the 10th of May, Windsor Castle was the backdrop for three brilliant evenings of military and equestrian displays, as well as music and dancing from around the world.

Before the performance began the Queen was presented with a special pair of African bracelets by Rose Kimanzi. The Queen laughed as Rose, who led a troupe of performers from Kenya, insisted she try on the handmade jewellery there and then. The bracelets were made by impoverished women at the charity where Rose works, near the Treetops lodge, where the Queen had been staying when she learned of the death of her father King George VI all those years ago.

The main event was staged inside the private grounds of Windsor Castle, where more than 550 horses and 1,000 performers created an unforgettable blaze of colour, sound and action.

The Queen has made more than 250 Commonwealth and state visits during her reign and, to celebrate this, the acts in the show came from every corner of the globe. Starting from London, the performers took spectators on a fabulous international journey, heading west and visiting the Americas, Australasia, Asia, the Middle East, Africa, Europe, and finishing back in Britain.

The entertainment was non-stop, from twirling Mexican dancers to Russian horse-riders, a flamboyant Maori troupe, Middle Eastern stunt riders and Indian folk legend Raghu Dixit.

The Queen is a well-known horse lover and it was clear she was enjoying every minute of the thrilling spectacle. With her were Prince Philip and other members of the Royal family including the Duke of York, Princess Beatrice, Prince and Princess Michael of Kent, Princess Alexandra and the Duchess of Cornwall.

The stars of stage and screen were also there to add their glamour to the event. Among the famous faces were actress Helen Mirren, singers Susan Boyle and Joss Stone, and Australian entertainer Rolf Harris. The event was narrated by Angela Rippon and Alan Titchmarsh.

The pageant included dancers and performers from all around the Commonwealth.

Armed Forces Parade and Muster at Windsor Castle

On 19 May nearly 3,000 troops from the Royal Navy, the Army and the Royal Air Force joined together in a spectacular military parade through Windsor. They mustered at the Castle, watched by the Queen, the Duke of Edinburgh, and members of the armed forces, their families and veterans.

At 11am nine RAF Typhoons flew low over Windsor Castle to start the event, then the half-mile long parade of immaculately attired military personnel began to file through the Castle's historic quadrangle. This intimate space was chosen to allow most of the troops to pass within just a few feet of the Queen. She was flanked by the Duke of Edinburgh and Chief of the Defence Staff, General Sir David Richards.

Six military bands provided a stirring soundtrack to the procession, playing several favourite pieces including *Rule Britannia* and *Land of Hope and Glory*, as well as new compositions. The event was concluded with a spectacular fly-past featuring 78 aircraft from all three forces. This included Lancasters, Spitfires, Hercules, VC10 and Tornado aircraft, as well as helicopters, Hawks, Tucanos and the Red Arrows.

^
Personnel from nearly all areas of the British Armed Forces parade in honour of Queen Elizabeth II during the Armed Forces Parade and Muster at Windsor Castle, 19 May 2012.

It is a long-standing tradition that the Armed Forces pay tribute to the monarch during a jubilee year. Queen Victoria's Diamond Jubilee in 1897 was marked with a Fleet Review at Spithead, Hampshire, and a Grand Military Tattoo at Windsor. King George V reviewed all three Forces (by then the RAF was in existence) separately for his Silver Jubilee in 1935.

The Queen did the same for her Silver Jubilee in 1977, while for her Golden Jubilee in 2002, the three Forces gathered for an event at Whale Island in Portsmouth. But this parade and muster in Windsor was the first time that all three Forces have visited the Queen for a dedicated event.

The Queen has long had a keen interest in the military. She was appointed honorary Colonel of the Grenadier Guards during World War II when still a 16-year-old princess. As monarch she is Commander-in-Chief of the Armed Forces, and her father, husband, two of her sons and two of her grandsons all served (or are serving) in the military.

^
The Queen, Prince Philip and Chief of the Defence Staff, General Sir David Richards (left), enjoy the show, including six military bands and a fly-past of nine RAF Typhoons.

The Diamond Jubilee Tour of Britain

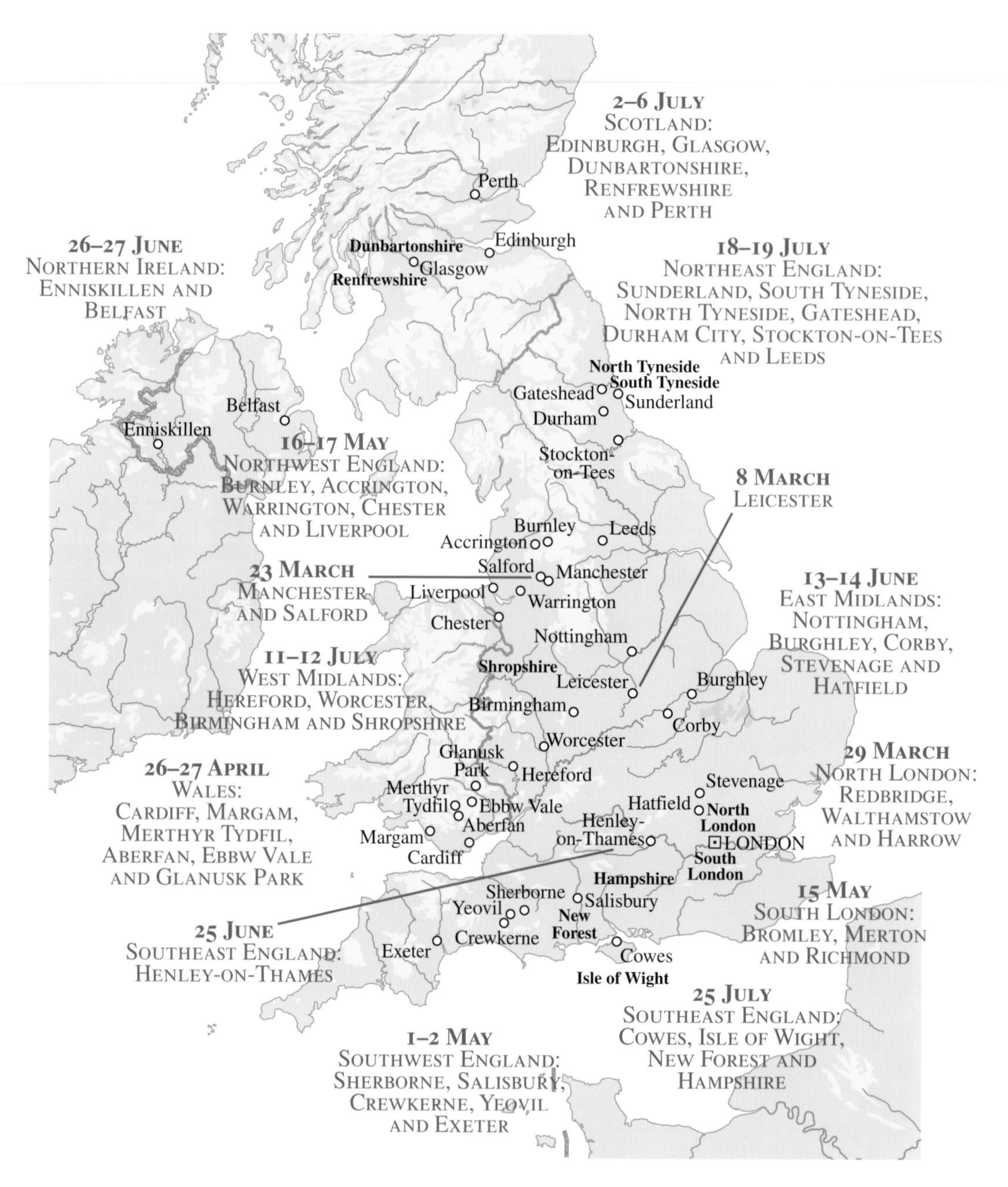

The Queen and Prince Philip visited dozens of towns and cities all over the United Kingdom in honour of the jubilee. Running from early March to late July, the Diamond Jubilee tour gave thousands of well-wishers the chance to show their appreciation of the Queen in person. She also used the visits to perform many historic civic duties.

The Queen started her tour at Leicester on 8 March where flag-waving crowds were standing three-deep to greet her. They had come early, armed with camping stools and flasks of hot tea, and when she arrived at the station there were whoops of joy and applause.

The Royal party travelled by motorcade to De Montfort University where spring sunshine added to the carnival atmosphere. There were stilt walkers, dancers and the streets were a sea of red, white and blue, with Union flags proudly displayed on banners, flags and smiling faces.

The Queen saw a display highlighting local charities and watched a fashion parade with the Duchess of Cambridge. Prince Philip viewed a local community project and the Royals later attended a service at Leicester Cathedral.

^
The Queen and the Duchess of Cambridge chat on the opening day of the monarch's Diamond Jubilee tour of Great Britain, in Leicester, 8 March 2012.

On 23 March the Queen and the Duke of Edinburgh stepped off the royal train at Victoria Station in Manchester to tumultuous applause from more than 800 flag-waving fans. They were met by 80 cadets and veterans from the Royal British Legion as musicians from Chetham's School of Music gave a rousing fanfare.

The Royal party chatted to well-wishers then headed to the Manchester Royal Eye Hospital on Oxford Road, where the Queen opened a £500m refurbishment project.

The Queen later opened the stunning new BBC studios and enjoyed watching *Football Focus* in rehearsal on a tour of the state-of-the-art facility. The Duke of Edinburgh inaugurated the university's new media centre. The Royal couple also took time to meet local community champions at Manchester Central conference hall.

^
A nasty surprise waits around the corner as the Queen tours the BBC studios, Manchester, 23 March.

The Queen and the Duke of Edinburgh began their visit to Cardiff on 26 April at a service in Llandaff Cathedral that celebrated her 60-year reign. At Margam Park they met the Welsh rugby team, who in March won their third *Grand Slam* in eight years. The party then flew by helicopter to Merthyr Tydfil where they enjoyed displays by the local mountain rescue team, Merthyr scouts and the Forestry Commission.

The next day the Queen visited Aberfan to open a new primary school. In 1966 a colliery spoil tip in the town collapsed, killing 144 people and virtually wiping out a generation in the community. The Queen has been deeply supportive of Aberfan since, visiting four times, and hundreds of well-wishers came to see her as she helped open a new chapter in the town's history. It was a poignant historic moment in what proved to be an unforgettable jubilee tour.

^
The Queen talks to parents bereaved by the 1966 Aberfan disaster, Gwyn and Sheila Lewis, during her visit to officially open Ynysowen Community Primary School in Aberfan, 27 April 2012.

Overseas trips by members of the Royal Family for the Jubilee

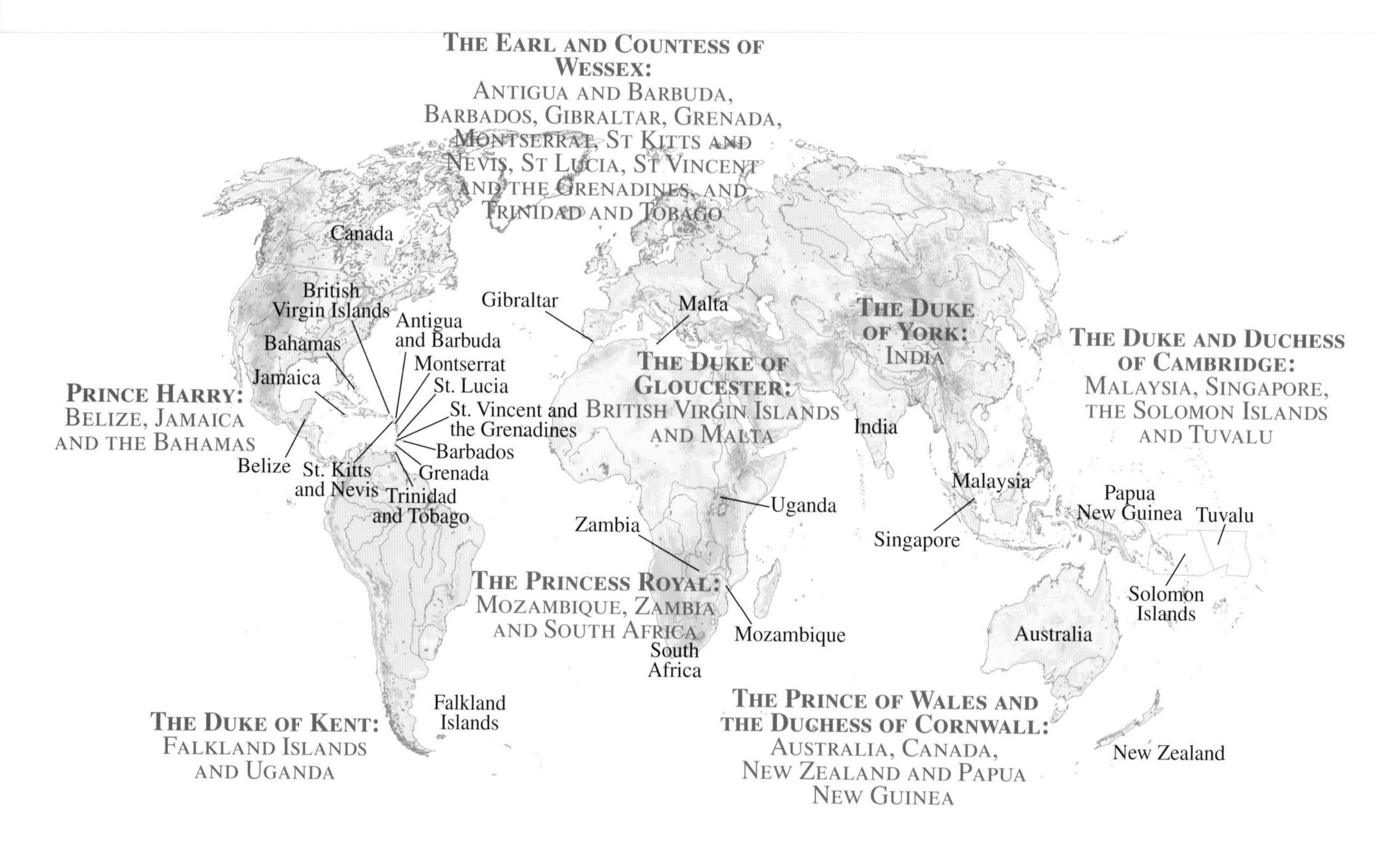

During the jubilee year, members of the Royal family travelled overseas to represent the Queen in many countries within the Commonwealth. The trips revealed how much of the world holds great affection for the Royal family.

The Prince of Wales and The Duchess of Cornwall: Australia, Canada, New Zealand, Papua New Guinea, Channel Islands, Isle of Man

Prince Charles and his wife the Duchess of Cornwall visited several UK cities in 2012. In Glasgow the Prince showed off his lighter side by presenting the weather forecast. This new 'career move' came during a tour of BBC Scotland's Pacific Quay headquarters when he stepped up to present *Reporting Scotland's* lunchtime weather forecast. When he read out the dismal prediction for Balmoral, he joked: 'Who the hell wrote this script?'

The sun may not have shone in Scotland, but the Prince and Duchess had an international tour of some rather warmer locations to look forward to, with Australia, Canada, New Zealand and Papua New Guinea all hosting the Royal couple later in the year.

Prince Charles first visited Papua New Guinea in 1966, during a school term spent at Timbertop School, an annexe of Geelong Grammar School in Australia (see page 55), as part of an exchange programme between Geelong and Gordonstoun. In his 45 years of Royal visits, the Prince has always been willing to get involved with local celebrations and traditions, and his 1966 trip had been no exception.

^
Prince Charles presents the weather on BBC Scotland's 'Reporting Scotland', 10 May 2012.

^
On his first trip to Papua New Guinea in 1966, Prince Charles joins in with the local customs.

The Duke and Duchess of Cambridge: Malaysia, Singapore, Solomon Islands, Tuvalu

In 2011 many people around the world celebrated the Royal wedding of Prince William and Catherine Middleton, now the Duke and Duchess of Cambridge. As many as 2 billion people worldwide watched the Westminster Abbey ceremony on 29 April, with 24.5 million watching live in the United Kingdom. The couple returned to their daily routines straight after the wedding, but in 2011 and 2012 they undertook several Royal visits.

Following the Christchurch earthquake in 2011, William had visited New Zealand and addressed the memorial service at Hagley Park on behalf of his grandmother. He then travelled to Australia, where he visited areas badly affected by flooding in the states of Queensland and Victoria.

The Duke and Duchess also toured Canada and the United States in June and July 2011, attending Canada Day celebrations on Parliament Hill. While in November the couple visited a UNICEF supply centre in Copenhagen, Denmark. They also dropped in on London's Centrepoint charity for the homeless, which the Duke has supported for many years, becoming patron in 2005.

For the Jubilee year, the Duke and Duchess had a scheduled overseas tour of Malaysia, Singapore, Solomon Islands, and Tuvalu. They also visited several UK destinations, including a very popular trip to Leicester with the Queen.

Part of the trip to Malaysia was planned to have particular meaning for the Duchess. She attended Marlborough College in Wiltshire, England and this highly regarded school has created its first overseas campus in Johor. The Duchess agreed to open this prestigious new development as part of her visit to the country.

1. Prince William surveys the damage to Christchurch Cathedral, caused by the earthquake that hit New Zealand's second largest city on the 22 February 2011; 2. The Prince meets Christchurch residents; 3. William and Catherine watch entertainers during the Calgary Stampede parade in Calgary, Alberta, Canada, 8 July 2011. >

THE DUKE OF YORK: INDIA

On 30 April, Prince Andrew flew to India for a seven-day visit, starting in New Delhi. He opened a 'Jubilee Walk' at the British High Commission and visited the Agragami Project, which is dedicated to improving the lives of some of Delhi's most vulnerable families. Later he attended a reception at the residence of the British High Commissioner to mark the Queen's Diamond Jubilee.

The next day the Duke laid a wreath at the Commonwealth War Graves Cemetery in Kohima, Nagaland, and attended a traditional Naga cultural show.

The mighty city of Mumbai was next, where he visited the Dharavi area, setting for the hit film *Slumdog Millionaire*, and home to some of the world's poorest people. He also met Indian Navy officers during a visit to the Indian Navy's INS *Viraat*.

In Kolkata, the Duke took time to a visit a child-care home and vocational education centre run by the Women's Interlink Foundation. He then headed to Chennai on 4 May to visit the Officers' Training Academy and lay a wreath at the Madras War Graves. He also attended a special Thanksgiving and Commemoration Service at St Mary's Church, Fort St George.

^
Prince Andrew, Duke of York, with school children during his visit to the Dhirubhai Ambani International School in Mumbai, 2 May 2012.

The Duke rounded off his trip by visiting the Governor of Karnataka in Bangalore and touring the headquarters of Infosys Technologies and Hindustan Aeronautics Limited.

The Earl and Countess of Wessex: Antigua and Barbuda, Barbados, Gibraltar, Grenada, Montserrat, St Kitts and Nevis, St Lucia, St Vincent and the Grenadines, Trinidad and Tobago.

In February and March, Prince Edward and his wife Sophie visited the Caribbean. Highlights of their tour included the 50th Anniversary Independence Day celebrations in St Lucia, a joint address from both houses of the Barbados Parliament and a visit to sites affected by the recent volcanic eruptions in Montserrat.

The tour began with the Royal couple arriving in Bridgetown, Barbados where Barbadian military personnel were given inspection. The Earl read a message from the Queen to a joint sitting of the Parliament of Barbados, which noted how much Barbados had achieved during its 45 years of independence, and called the country a model small state for others around the world.

The following day, the Countess visited the Albert C. Graham Children's Development Centre, while the Earl presented eight Duke of Edinburgh's Gold Awards to Barbadian young people at a dedication ceremony.

The Earl and Countess of Wessex participated in Independence Day celebrations in St Lucia on 21 February. On 3 March they enjoyed historical re-enactments and cultural shows in St Kitts and Nevis, and also visited the children's ward of a local hospital before attending a state dinner and fireworks display at Port Zante.

Prince Harry: Belize, Jamaica, The Bahamas

In Belize, the Governor-General and the Belize Tourism Board organised a tour of the country for Prince Harry, between 2 and 3 March 2012, as part of the country's celebrations of Elizabeth II's 60th year as monarch of Belize, first as Queen of the United Kingdom and then, after 1981, as Queen of Belize.

In the capital city of Belmopan, Prince Harry unveiled a series of commemorative stamps issued by the Belize Postal Service. He then attended the city's street festival, dedicating a street as *Queen Elizabeth II Boulevard*, and delivering a speech on the sovereign's behalf.

The Prince visited Xunantunich where he met children involved with the Belize Special Olympics Programme, and presented a canoe to the Ruta Maya Organization in commemoration of the Diamond Jubilee. Prince Harry further visited the Price Barracks and laid a wreath at the monument to British soldiers killed while on service in Belize.

Prince Harry toured Jamaica between 5 and 8 March 2012, taking part in military exercises with the Jamaica Defence Force and visiting Bustamante Hospital for Children.

During his tour the relaxed and fun-loving prince took part in a Diamond Jubilee street party and showed off his dancing skills in Belize. He also formally honoured the Queen at a thanksgiving service in The Bahamas. He attended a reception for youth leaders and met with the Governor-General of the Bahamas Sir Arthur Foulkes. The Prince attended an outdoor ceremony where children's schools, clubs, and associations presented themselves.

Perhaps the most memorable event of the Prince's trip was his meeting with champion sprinter Usain Bolt at the latter's training ground at the University of the West Indies, at Mona, Jamaica. Despite Bolt being the world 100m and 200m record holder, Harry managed to 'beat' him – albeit by starting running before anyone said 'go'!

A 'Jamaica Night' reception was held at the Royal Caribbean Hotel in Montego Bay, and Governor-General of Jamaica Sir Patrick Allen hosted a dinner at King's House as a combined celebration of the Diamond Jubilee and Jamaica's 50th anniversary of independence. The Prime Minister, Portia Simpson Miller, stated that the tour was intended to 'highlight the country's tourism developments on the North Coast and the important work being done in the area of youth and children.'

Overall, Prince Harry's Caribbean tour was a triumph. The 27-year-old Prince had been astounded by the warm reception he received and by the way the countries celebrated the Queen's 60-year reign on what he called 'an emotional trip'.

^
Prince Harry prepares to 'race' Usain Bolt at the Usain Bolt Track, the University of the West Indies, Jamaica, 6 March 2012.

THE PRINCESS ROYAL: MOZAMBIQUE, ZAMBIA, SOUTH AFRICA

The Princess Royal visited Mozambique, Zambia and South Africa with her husband Timothy Laurence as part of the Queen's Diamond Jubilee celebrations.

The Princess Royal's two-day visit to Mozambique saw her dropping in on community projects particularly close to her heart. At Save the Children's Community Project in Gobo Gobo, she saw first-hand how the charity is giving children a headstart in life by teaching them everyday skills such as cooking, sewing, painting, and arts and crafts.

The Princess is a patron of Opportunity International, a UK-based charity that helps millions of people in the developing world by offering them small loans, savings and insurance schemes. In Mozambique, the Princess Royal visited a mobile bank unit to talk to some of the local people who have used one of its small loans to start a business and build their own livelihoods.

Princess Anne also attended a reception in Chimoio that showed how UK organizations are helping local people in Manica province. These British companies and NGOs (non-governmental organizations) are closely involved with the development of local agriculture, improving seed quality and bringing expertise to many specialist fields, such as honey production. These organizations have been instrumental in revitalizing the economy and attracting more investments to the area.

Another highlight was her visit to the International Inspiration Project. Most children love sport, and this scheme uses games and activities to enrich the lives of millions of children. Active in Mozambique since 2009, it enjoyed a substantial boost in 2012, thanks to the London Olympics and the Princess Royal's inspiring visit.

The Duke of Gloucester: British Virgin Islands, Malta

In March the Queen's cousin, Prince Richard, Duke of Gloucester, toured the British Virgin Islands. On Tortola, he met participants in the Sailability BVI programme, including Special Olympics medallists, and visited the headquarters of the Virgin Islands search and rescue service. His jubilee year duties also included a visit to Malta.

The Duke of Kent: Falkland Islands, Uganda

The Duke of Kent made two overseas trips in honour of his cousin the Queen's jubilee year, to the Falkland Islands and Uganda. He also performed a number of special duties in the UK, including opening the new wing at Sunderland Royal Hospital on 3 April. This new wing will be formally known as 'The Jubilee Wing'.

^
Princess Anne speaks to school children at the Soweto Equestrian foundation in Soweto, South Africa, 16 April 2012.

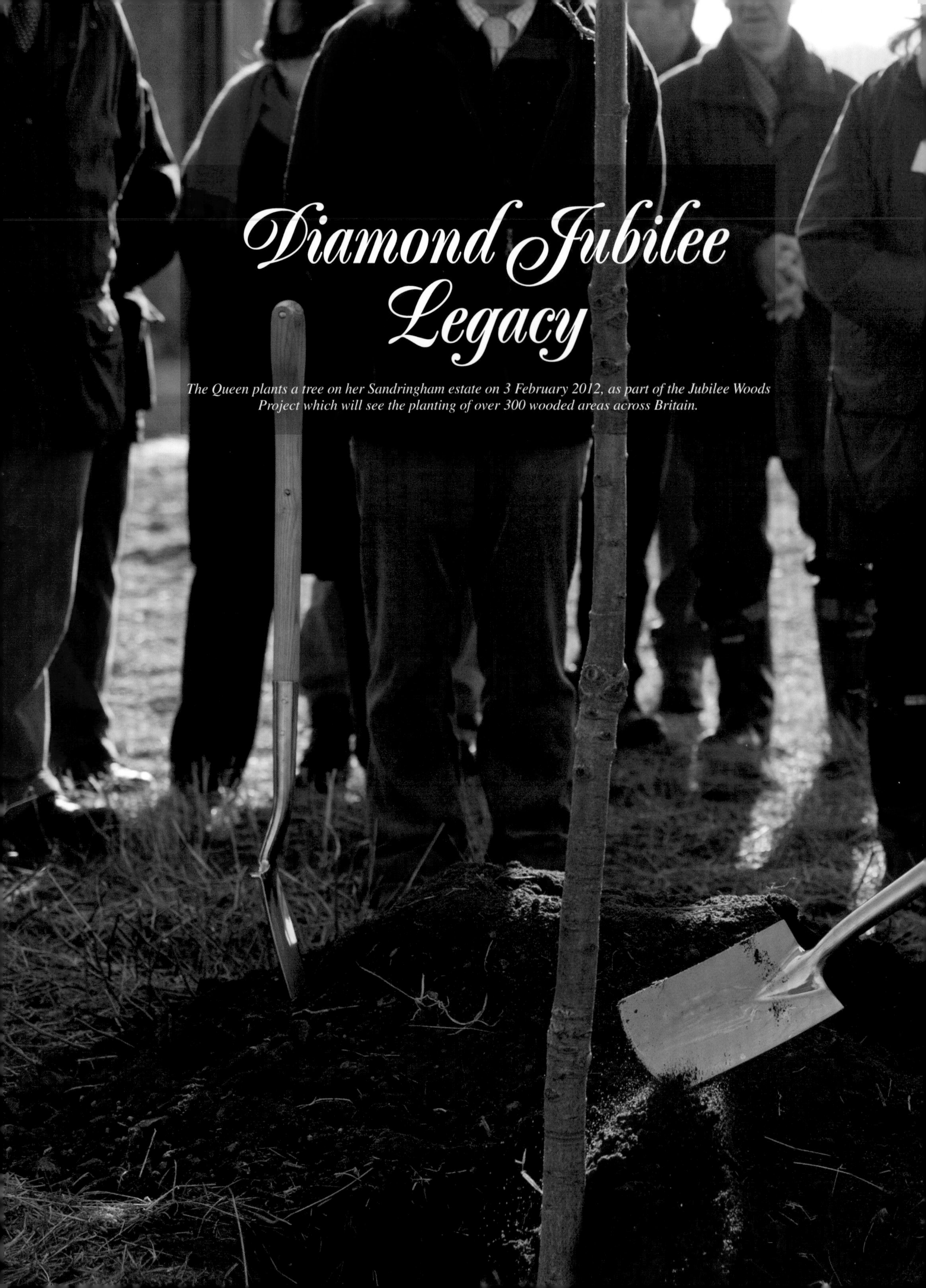

Diamond Jubilee Legacy

The Queen plants a tree on her Sandringham estate on 3 February 2012, as part of the Jubilee Woods Project which will see the planting of over 300 wooded areas across Britain.

Diamond Jubilee Legacy

The Queen celebrates her Diamond Jubilee as the second-longest serving monarch in 1,000 years of British history. More than that, she is Queen to more than 2 billion people living in 16 Commonwealth Realms, and Head of the Commonwealth of 54 independent countries. It is, by any measure, an historic reign, and her achievements will continue to endure far into the future. In recognition of this, many individuals and organizations throughout the Commonwealth have united in creative and inspiring ways to celebrate her legacy in the years to come. Just a few of these remarkable projects are showcased here.

The Jubilee Woods Project

In the 60 years of her reign the Queen has planted countless trees to mark significant occasions. It is fitting then that to help celebrate her legacy the Woodland Trust launched the Jubilee Woods Project, one of the largest tree-planting campaigns ever undertaken. The patron of the project is the Princess Royal.

With the help of nearly a million volunteers, the Trust created more than 300 Jubilee Woods throughout the country. Of these, 60 are Diamond Woods – each at least a 60-acre woodland specially planted to pay tribute to a year of the Queen's reign. So many organizations joined in with the scheme that the Woodland Trust created another 25 Princess Woods to mark the years before the Queen's Accession. The centrepiece of the Jubilee Woods Project is the 460-acre Diamond Wood in the heart of The National Forest in Leicestershire, containing over 300,000 trees.

The woods will contain 420 native species, including 'Royal Oak' grown from saplings collected on Royal estates. They will transform the British landscape, creating new sanctuaries for wildlife, places for reflection and play, and providing a magnificent tribute to the Queen for generations to come.

The Queen's Diamond Jubilee Volunteering Award 2012

The Queen's Diamond Jubilee Volunteering Award for 2012 will recognize national volunteer organizations, as well as organizations which have been and will continue to work with volunteers as part of the Olympic and Paralympic Games. The Award demonstrates recognition by the Queen of the immensely valuable work done by volunteers in the UK.

The Queen Elizabeth Diamond Jubilee Trust

In 2011, the Commonwealth Heads of Government announced the establishment of The Queen Elizabeth Diamond Jubilee Trust, which would accept charitable donations from individuals, groups and organizations for the duration of the Jubilee year, under the chairmanship of former prime minister Sir John Major.

The Trust was officially launched on 6 February 2012, the 60th anniversary of the Queen's Accession. Donations of all sizes came flooding in, from pocket-money pennies to generous government and business bequests.

For five years, the Trust will work with partner charities and organizations to deliver projects aimed at improving the lives of many of the individuals and communities across the Commonwealth.

The projects are based on six themes: *Young Diamonds*, aimed at helping young people to improve their lives and communities through the use of sports-based events and activities; *Urban Food*, encouraging communities to grow their own food for consumption and for selling; *Disability to Capability*, helping people with disabilities to be active members of their communities; *Heritage and Culture*, using modern technology to trace the history and share the cultural heritage of different ethnic groups; *Exceptional Leaders*, identifying and supporting 60 individuals to develop projects to improve the well-being of their communities; and *Care with Dignity*, a programme helping older people to lead active lives and to remain valued members of their communities.

Diamond Jubilee stamps and coins

Over the last six decades, the Queen's likeness has become one of the most recognizable and reproduced in the world, appearing on billions of coins and stamps. The Royal Mail created a unique set of six stamps to mark the 60th anniversary of the Queen's Accession to the throne. The issue was a philatelic first: it featured official portraits of the Queen from previous stamps, as well as from coins and banknotes. These include society photographer Dorothy Wilding's portrait of the Queen, which was used on the very first stamp issued during her reign, and portraits taken from the £1 banknote issued in 1960.

Diamond Jubilee UK £5 Coin

The Royal Mint has created a special £5 coin, which has the distinction of being the first coin ever struck to commemorate a diamond jubilee – it was a medal, rather than a coin, that was created in honour of Queen Victoria's 60 years on the throne.

The coin features two new portraits of the Queen, between them spanning the 60 years of her reign. The modern depiction on the obverse shows her crowned and wearing the formal robes of the Order of the Garter, while the reverse bears a portrait of the young Queen Elizabeth wearing a laurel crown, which is reminiscent of the first coinage to be produced during her reign, in 1953. The coin also features the Latin words *Dirige Deus Gressus Meos* – May God Guide My Steps – which appeared on the gold £5 coin of 1839.

New Jubilee Cities

In time-honoured jubilee tradition, local authorities were invited to submit bids to the deputy prime minister's office for their towns to be awarded city status. The accolade is purely honorific and confers no additional powers, functions or funding, but the prestige of being granted the award was eagerly pursued by 26 towns. Under royal prerogative, the Queen granted city status to Chelmsford in Essex, Perth in Perthshire and St Asaph in Denbighshire. The three new cities therefore represent the home countries, featuring one each from England, Scotland and Wales. Armagh in Northern Ireland, already a city, was given the honour of having a lord mayor.

Chelmsford is an important centre in the political life of Essex and has been the county town since 1215. Chelmsford Cathedral was first built as the church of St Mary the Virgin around the same time.

Known as the *Fair City*, Perth sits on the banks of the River Tay, Scotland's longest river. Its new status makes it Scotland's seventh city.

With only 3,400 residents, St Asaph is the second smallest city in the UK after St David's. Its beautiful cathedral dates to the 13th century.

Greenwich becomes a Royal Borough

The borough of Greenwich, in southeast London, has enjoyed close links with royalty since the Middle Ages. It is home to several former Royal residences, including Eltham Palace, once a Royal nursery for the use of Henry VII's children. It also has many buildings with Royal status including the Old Royal Naval College, which was built on the site of the old Greenwich Palace where Elizabeth I, Mary I and Henry VIII were born.

In 2012 it joined a very exclusive group when it became only the fourth local authority to become a Royal borough and the first new one for more than 80 years. The new regal status is similar to a person being awarded an honour, but with even more exclusivity: the only others members of the club are Kensington and Chelsea, Windsor and Maidenhead, and Kingston-upon-Thames. The new legal status was made official with a Royal Charter signed by the Queen.

The accolade was also made in recognition of the borough's global significance as the home of the Prime Meridian, Greenwich Mean Time, and as a UNESCO World Heritage Site.

A new Royal coat of arms has taken pride of place on signs on the streets of the southeast London borough. It features a Tudor rose, for which special dispensation was granted, to represent the area's long association with royalty. New signs with the emblem will replace old ones as they wear out.

The Queen Elizabeth II Fields Challenge

The Queen Elizabeth II Fields Challenge, or as it is known in Scotland, the Queen Elizabeth Fields Challenge, is a campaign that will protect 2,012 outdoor recreational spaces in communities all across the country as a permanent living legacy of this historic year. The challenge is spearheaded by its patron, the Duke of Cambridge.

From formal gardens in the heart of the city to suburban parks and the wider countryside, recreational spaces are often at the heart of any community. By regenerating existing spaces and inaugurating new ones, the Queen Elizabeth II Fields Challenge seeks to ensure that more 'green lungs' breathe life into the land for future generations. By protecting a diverse range of community spaces, the Challenge will ensure that there is a recreational haven that appeals to everyone.

^
Prince William plays rugby with children as he visits Eden Park Stadium, Auckland, New Zealand.

Throughout 2012, communities voted for a beloved local space to become part of the scheme and be permanently protected as a tribute to the Diamond Jubilee. The open spaces themselves come in all shapes and sizes: woodlands, bicycle trails, children's play areas, parks and sports pitches. Encouraging outdoor activity and sport at grassroots level was particularly relevant given the other milestone event in the UK in 2012 – the London Olympics. Now communities the length and breadth of the country will have a lasting and positive legacy of the Diamond Jubilee woven into the fabric of their everyday lives.

The 60 'New Elizabethans'

The Queen has met thousands of the people in her years as a public figure, from politicians to pop stars, emperors to everyday people. Many of these may be considered to define the years of her reign.

To mark the Diamond Jubilee, broadcaster James Naughtie invited the British public to nominate the public figures who have made the greatest impact in Britain during the Queen's reign: the men and women whose deeds will stand the test of time. The nominees could be in any field and all the names put forward were passed to a panel of historians who debated and decided on the final list of 60. Radio 4 then broadcast profiles of each of the chosen New Elizabethans throughout the summer of 2012.

The final list included some of the most significant achievers of the previous six decades from various fields including politics, sport, the arts, education, and the media. Controversially, the list included less well-known figures, along with some pretty unpopular ones, who the judges believed had influenced the period as much as or often more than the 'heroes' from the shortlist.

The final 60 'New Elizabethans' were:

Edmund Hillary
Elizabeth David
Graham Greene
Michael Young
Vladimir Raitz
Doris Lessing
Alan Sainsbury
Alfred Hitchcock
Laurence Olivier
Benjamin Britten
Dorothy Hodgkin
Harold Pinter
Richard Doll
Tony Hancock
Philip Larkin
Barbara Windsor
Lord Denning
Paul Foot
Francis Bacon
John Lennon and Paul McCartney
Margot Fonteyn
Peter Hall
Terence Conran
Enoch Powell
Cicely Saunders
Basil D'Oliveira
George Best
Germaine Greer
Robert Edwards
Jack Jones
Roald Dahl
David Bowie
Talaisai Labalaba
Jocelyn Bell Burnell
Roy Jenkins
Vivienne Westwood
Jayaben Desai
Stuart Hall
David Attenborough
Margaret Thatcher
David Hockney
Billy Connolly
Ralph Robins
Amartya Sen
Salman Rushdie
Anita Roddick
Norman Foster
Charles Saatchi
Goldie
John Hume and David Trimble
Doreen Lawrence
Tim Berners-Lee
Diana, Princess of Wales
Alex Salmond
Tony Blair
Fred Goodwin
Rupert Murdoch
Simon Cowell

Diamond Jubilee Celebrations

The Queen, Camilla, Duchess of Cornwall, and Prince Charles, Prince of Wales, leave Westminster Hall in the 1902 State Landau at the start of a carriage procession to Buckingham Palace, as part of the Queen's Diamond Jubilee celebration weekend, London, 5 June 2012.

Diamond Jubilee Celebrations

For four days in early June much of London, Britain and the Commonwealth came to a virtual standstill for a series of celebratory events that together constituted an unforgettable Diamond Jubilee weekend.

To start the weekend, the anniversary of Her Majesty Queen Elizabeth II's Coronation on Saturday, 2 June 2012 was marked by a 41-gun Royal Salute in Horse Guards Parade, London, fired by The King's Troop Royal Horse Artillery. Other salutes were simultaneously fired at other locations in the UK, including the Tower of London, Edinburgh, Belfast and Cardiff.

Derby Day

Around 130,000 fans of racing and royalty were at the Epsom Derby on Saturday for the first major event of the Diamond Jubilee weekend. The course was kitted out with Union flags and the Queen's standard flew above the grandstand. As well

^
Tom Queally (centre) riding Wrotham Heath on his way to winning The Diamond Jubilee Handicap.

as the Derby, the race-card for the day included the Diamond Jubilee Coronation Cup and the Diamond Jubilee Handicap.

Members of the Red Devils aerobatics team set the celebratory tone for the day when they parachuted on to the racecourse with a huge Union flag.

The Queen and the Duke of Edinburgh then arrived and toured the course in a Royal motorcade before sitting down to enjoy the races. The Queen is a known lover of all things equestrian, and her pleasure at the day's events was there for all to see.

Welsh mezzo-sporano Katherine Jenkins sang the national anthem to the crowd, accompanied by the band of Her Majesty's Royal Marines.

^
1. The Red Devils drop in at Epsom Racecourse with a huge Union flag, 2 June 2012; 2. The Queen and Prince Philip arrive at Epsom for the Derby meeting; 3. Katherine Jenkins sings the national anthem before the start of the racing.

Big Jubilee Lunch

On Sunday 3 June, nearly 10,000 streets became rivers of red, white and blue as people all over the UK took to the open air to share lunch with neighbours and friends in street parties and picnics to commemorate the Jubilee.

The capital hosted some of the most spectacular celebrations with the Big Jubilee Lunch turning the normally traffic-filled thoroughfare of Piccadilly into one long line of tables. This al fresco feast took on a particularly royal flavour when the Duke and Duchess of Cornwall arrived for a bite and chat with some of the revellers.

The street parties seemed to bring out the best of the British sense of fun and eccentricity. Party-goers in Bristol's Millennium Square could 'make their own corgi' and the food on offer in Richmond Park in Gainsborough was pegged at 1952 prices. Hot dogs cost just 7 pence, bacon sandwiches 9 pence and a cup of tea only 2 pence.

^
The Duke and Duchess of Cornwall enjoy the street party atmosphere.

The Thames Diamond Jubilee Pageant

The very British drizzle didn't dampen the spirits of the 1.2 million people who gathered along the banks and bridges of the River Thames on Sunday 3 June for the Diamond Jubilee Pageant.

The river was brought jubilantly to life with the largest flotilla ever assembled. Around 1,000 working boats and pleasure vessels of all shapes and sizes began gathering early in the morning, decked in red, white and blue and with their crews turned out in their finest rigs. Many boats had travelled long distances to represent UK port cities, the Commonwealth countries and other international interests.

The pageant started at Wandsworth Bridge, passing 14 Thames bridges before finishing at Tower Bridge. The procession of boats was 7.5 miles (12.1 km) long and was formed in five sections, each with its own 'herald barges' that carried a band. The final barge carried the London Philharmonic Orchestra.

The pageant's lead vessel was a floating belfry with a new set of eight church bells cast at the Whitechapel Bell Foundry especially for the Diamond Jubilee celebrations. The Queen, Prince Philip, the Duke and Duchess of Cornwall, Princes William and Harry and the Duchess of Cambridge were aboard the Royal Barge, *Spirit of Chartwell*. Decked out in a fine red, gold and purple colour scheme, this vessel was clearly inspired by the elegant royal barges of the 17th and 18th centuries. On its prow was a gilded sculpture of Old Father Thames, with a pair of dolphins and the Royal cipher at the centre.

Other notable craft included the row barge *Gloriana*, which was powered by 18 oarsmen including Olympians Sir Steve Redgrave and Sir Matthew Pinsent. Boris Johnson, London mayor, was on *The Havengore*, the vessel that bore Winston Churchill's coffin in 1965.

L M S
6201
1
2
3
4

As the boats approached each bridge, great waves of cheers rose up from the spectators, reaching a crescendo as the Royal Barge approached. Despite the rain, the 86-year-old Queen stood on the *Spirit of Chartwell* for nearly four hours, waving and acknowledging the salutes of the spectators until the end of the procession.

Near Tower Bridge the Queen was saluted by the guns, the naval cadets and veterans aboard the HMS *Belfast* and the Royal Barge docked at HMS *President*. When the orchestra drew up along the Royal Barge, they played the *Hornpipe*, which set many toes tapping and umbrellas bobbing. This was followed with *Rule Britannia* and *God Save the Queen*. The bascules of the bridge lowered, the craft on the river sounded their horns and fireworks signed off this utterly unique pageant.

Jubilee Concert

Music was in the air on the evening of Monday 4 June, thanks to the highly entertaining three-hour Jubilee Concert in front of Buckingham Palace, organized by Take That's Gary Barlow. More than 1.2 million applications were received for the 10,000 free concert tickets.

The first half of the concert, held before the Queen took her seat, focused on contemporary pop. Robbie Williams started proceedings with his usual pomp, including the Guards drummers and trumpeters on his song *Let Me Entertain You*. Other artists including Jessie J, will.i.am, Annie Lennox, Grace Jones, and JLS kept fans' feet tapping.

Sir Cliff Richard was first of four knights to play, getting all the audience singing along to *Congratulations*. Sir Tom Jones inspired a mass flamenco dance on the steps of the Queen Victoria Memorial during *Delilah*, and Sir Elton John gave a touching

< 1. The Princess Elizabeth steam locomotive whistles at the start of the Thames River Pageant, as the Royal Britannia tender carries the Queen and Prince Philip to the Royal Barge; 2. The Royal party all elect to stand rather than sit for the ride on the Royal Barge, Spirit of Chartwell; 3. The Spirit of Chartwell; 4. Row barge Gloriana leads the flotilla under Lambeth Bridge.

performance of *Your Song*. Sir Paul McCartney sang several classics including *Let It Be* and *Live And Let Die*, which sparked a spectacular firework display.

When the Queen did arrive, it was without the Duke of Edinburgh, who had earlier been taken to hospital, suffering from a bladder infection. Perhaps the crowd sensed that she was missing him, because they broke into an impromptu chant of 'Philip, Philip' and the Queen appeared visibly moved by the crowd's enthusiastic support. She then enjoyed memorable performances from the likes of Dame Shirley Bassey, Kylie Minogue, Rolf Harris and Madness, who performed on the roof of the Palace with lead singer Suggs cheekily changing the lyrics to the band's song *Our House* to *One's house*.

The sound and light spectacular proved to be a proper Royal knees-up, with Princesses Eugenie and Beatrice seen dancing in their seats to Jessie J, Prince Harry particularly enjoying Kylie's performance, and Prince William rocking along with Sir Paul.

^ *William and Kate enjoy the show.*

Performers at the Jubilee Concert: >
1. Kylie Minogue; 2. Madness; 3. Sir Paul McCartney; 4. Peter Kay; 5. Stevie Wonder.

1
2
3
4
5
VOX

Blazing into History

A network of beacons is Britain's oldest signalling system, long used to mobilize the militia during threats such as the attack by the Spanish Armada. Commemorative beacons have also been lit for many hundreds of years for Royal weddings, jubilees and coronations. Beacons were lit to celebrate Queen Victoria's Diamond Jubilee in 1897 and the same was done in 1977 and 2002 for the Queen's Silver and Golden Jubilees.

To mark the Queen's Diamond Jubilee, the aim was to have 2,012 beacons worldwide, but twice that many were created, the most ever for such an occasion. They were built in every corner of the Commonwealth, from village greens and farms to front gardens and beaches, church towers and castle battlements – even mountain peaks.

The first Diamond Jubilee beacon was lit in Tonga by local scouts and girl guides, long before darkness reached the UK. The cascade of light then rippled westwards round the world. Other beacon sites included the Treetops hotel in Kenya, where the young Princess Elizabeth heard that her father, King George VI, had died in 1952. At 10.30pm after the concert at Buckingham Palace, the Queen placed the Jubilee Crystal Diamond into a special pod to light the final beacon in The Mall.

^
Reverend Jane Hedges, Canon of Westminster Abbey, lights a beacon outside the Abbey as part of the Diamond Jubilee celebrations, 4 June 2012.

Service Of Thanksgiving

The final day of the Diamond Jubilee weekend was marked by a national service of thanksgiving at St Paul's Cathedral. The Queen was greeted as she arrived at the cathedral by a fanfare and jubilant crowds chanting 'God save the Queen'. During the service the Archbishop of Canterbury praised her 'lifelong dedication' to the service of her nation and the Commonwealth, and Prime Minister David Cameron gave a reading. Many international leaders were in attendance and US President Barack Obama later paid the Queen a special tribute, calling her 'a steadfast ally, loyal friend and tireless leader'.

After the service at St Paul's, the Queen attended a reception at nearby Mansion House, the official residence of the Lord Mayor of London, while the Prince of Wales and Duchess of Cornwall, the Duke and Duchess of Cambridge and Prince Harry attended a similar event at the Guildhall.

^
The Royal family join in the hymns at St Paul's during the Jubilee thanksgiving service, 5 June 2012.

Royal Procession

The senior Royals then attended a Diamond Jubilee lunch at Westminster Hall organized by the Livery – although once again Prince Philip was unable to attend due to illness – before processing back to Buckingham Palace in the final set-piece event of the Jubilee weekend. The Queen rode in an open-topped coach with the Prince of Wales and the Duchess of Cornwall. Princes William and Harry and the Duchess of Cambridge followed in

^
The Queen with Camilla, Duchess of Cornwall, Prince Harry and Prince William with Catherine, Duchess of Cambridge, take part in the carriage procession back to Buckingham Palace

a second coach. The route was lined with thousands of cheering well-wishers waving Union flags.

The procession was led along The Mall by soldiers from the Household Cavalry Mounted Regiment. A 60-gun salute was fired by the King's Troop, Royal Horse Artillery. The Queen and other senior Royals then came out onto the balcony of Buckingham Palace to acknowledge the respect of the huge crowds, which were now numbered in the hundreds of thousands. The whole show was brought to a close with a fly-past by World War II aircraft, including a Lancaster and Spitfires, accompanied by the Red Arrows.

It was a thrilling and fitting climax to a remarkable Diamond Jubilee weekend that celebrated the 60 year reign of a remarkable monarch: Her Majesty Queen Elizabeth II.

^
The crowd surges into The Mall, to watch the fly-past and see the final balcony appearance.

The Jubilee weekend officially finishes with a fly-past of World War II planes, as the Queen appears on the balcony with Princes Charles, William and Harry, and the Duchesses of Cornwall and Cambridge. >

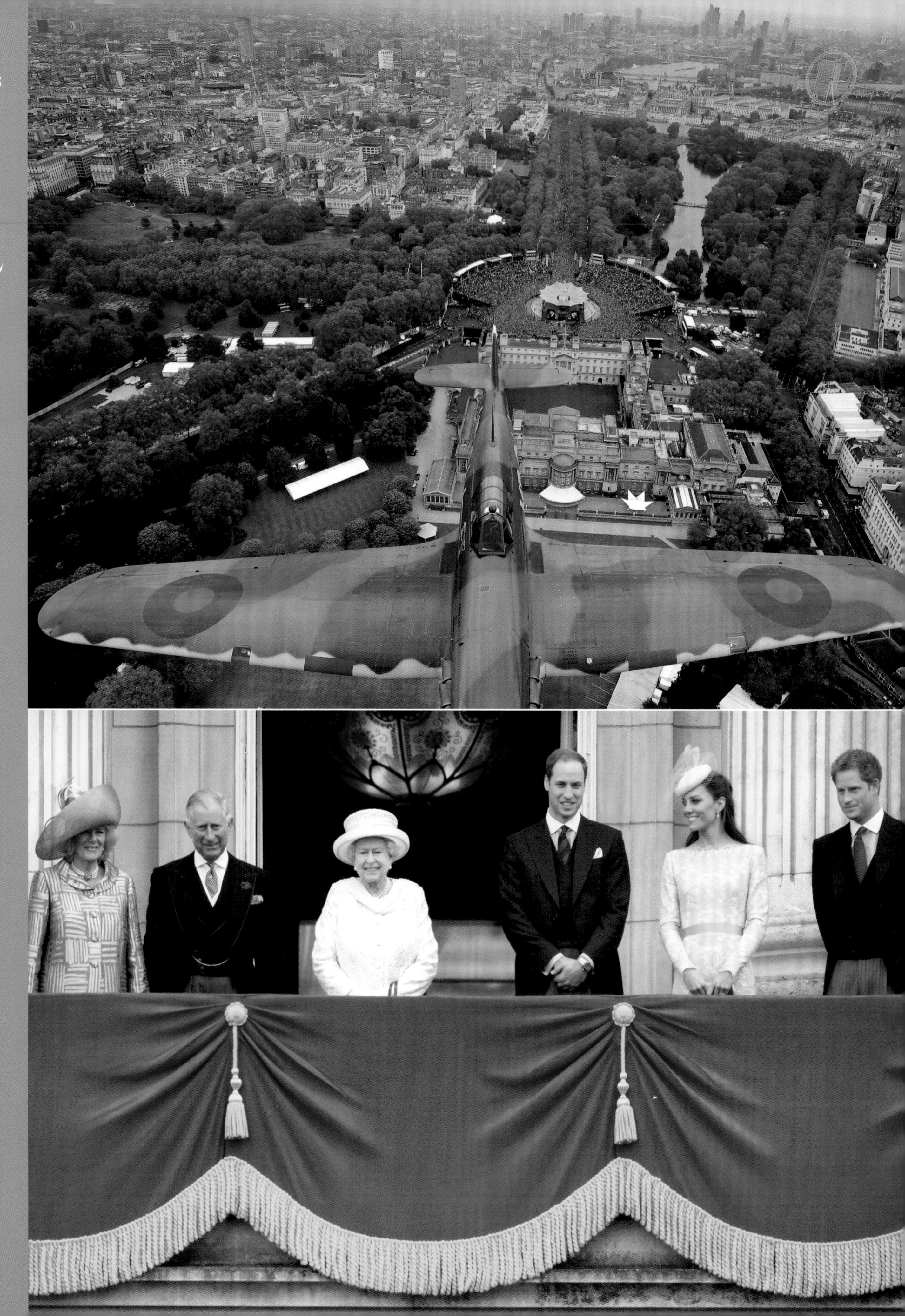

Image Credits:

6 Getty Images
8 Getty Images
9 Getty Images
10 Popperfoto/Getty Images
11 (bl) Getty Images
11 Popperfoto/Getty Images
11 Popperfoto/Getty Images
11 Popperfoto/Getty Images
11 Getty Images
13 Getty Images
14 Getty Images
15 Popperfoto/Getty Images
16 Popperfoto/Getty Images
17 Getty Images
19 (1) Popperfoto/Getty Images
19 (2) Time & Life Pictures/Getty Images
19 (3) Getty Images
19 (4) Getty Images
19 (5) Popperfoto/Getty Images
19 (6) Gamma-Keystone via Getty Images
22 Time & Life Pictures/Getty Images
24 Getty Images
26 Popperfoto/Getty Images
27 Time & Life Pictures/Getty Images
28 (l) Popperfoto/Getty Images
28 (r) Getty Images
29 Getty Images
31 AFP/Getty Images
32 Getty Images
33 Popperfoto/Getty Images
35 (1) AFP/Getty Images
35 Getty Images
35 Getty Images
35 (4) Popperfoto/Getty Images
35 Getty Images
37 AFP/Getty Images
38 Popperfoto/Getty Images
40 Getty Images
42 Getty Images
43 Getty Images
44 Getty Images
45 Popperfoto/Getty Images
47 (l) Getty Images
47 (r) Time & Life Pictures/Getty Images
49 Getty Images
49 Getty Images
49 Getty Images
49 Getty Images
50 Popperfoto/Getty Images
51 Popperfoto/Getty Images
52 Popperfoto/Getty Images
54 Getty Images
56 (l) Getty Images
56 (r) Gamma-Keystone via Getty Images
56 (b) Popperfoto/Getty Images
57 Getty Images
58 Getty Images
59 Getty Images
60 Popperfoto/Getty Images
61 Getty Images
65 Popperfoto/Getty Images
66 Getty Images
68 Getty Images
70 Getty Images
71 Getty Images
72 Getty Images
75 (1) Tim Graham/Getty Images
75 (2) Gamma-Keystone via Getty Images
75 (3) Getty Images
75 (4) Getty Images
75 (5) Tim Graham/Getty Images
77 Getty Images
78 Getty Images
81 Getty Images
81 (2) Time & Life Pictures/Getty Images
81 Getty Images
81 (4) Tim Graham/Getty Images
82 Tim Graham/Getty Images
85 Tim Graham/Getty Images
86 Getty Images
87 Tim Graham/Getty Images
88 (fade) Patricia Hofmeester/Shutterstock
89 (l) Rod Edwards
89 (r) Getty Images
91 (1) AFP/Getty Images
91 Popperfoto/Getty Images
91 (3) Tim Graham/Getty Images
91 Popperfoto/Getty Images
91 (5) Getty Images
93 Getty Images
95 Tim Graham/Getty Images
97 (1) Tim Graham/Getty Images
97 Getty Images
97 Getty Images
98 Tim Graham/Getty Images
101 Tim Graham/Getty Images
102 Tim Graham/Getty Images
103 Tim Graham/Getty Images
105 (1) AFP/Getty Images
105 Tim Graham/Getty Images
105 Tim Graham/Getty Images
105 Tim Graham/Getty Images
107 AFP/Getty Images
108 Tim Graham/Getty Images
109 AFP/Getty Images
110 (l) AFP/Getty Images
110 (r) Tim Graham/Getty Images
112 (1) Tim Graham/Getty Images
112 Getty Images
112 Getty Images
112 (4) AFP/Getty Images
112 Getty Images
112 Getty Images
114 AFP/Getty Images
114 AFP/Getty Images
115 (t) Getty Images
115 (b) Time & Life Pictures/Getty Images
116 Tim Graham/Getty Images
118 Getty Images
119 Tim Graham/Getty Images
120 AFP/Getty Images
121 AFP/Getty Images
122 Tim Graham/Getty Images
123 Getty Images
125 (1) AFP/Getty Images
125 (2) LOCOG
125 Getty Images
125 Getty Images
125 Getty Images
125 Getty Images
127 Tim Graham/Getty Images
128 Tim Graham/Getty Images
129 (t) AFP/Getty Images
129 (b) Getty Images
130 Getty Images
131 Getty Images
132 AFP/Getty Images
135 Getty Images
135 Getty Images
135 Getty Images
135 Getty Images
135 (5) AFP/Getty Images
136 Getty Images
139 Getty Images
140 AFP/Getty Images
141 AFP/Getty Images
143 Getty Images
143 Getty Images
143 Getty Images
143 Getty Images
143 Getty Images
144 Getty Images
144 Getty Images
146 Getty Images
147 Getty Images
148 Getty Images
149 Getty Images
149 Getty Images
149 Getty Images
151 Getty Images
152 Getty Images
153 Getty Images
155 (t) Getty Images
155 (b) Tim Graham/Getty Images
157 Getty Images
157 Getty Images
157 (3) AFP/Getty Images
158 India Today Group/Getty Images
160 Getty Images
161 Getty Images
163 Getty Images
164 Getty Images
171 Getty Images
173 Atlaspix/Shutterstock
174 AFP/Getty Images
176 Getty Images
177 Getty Images
177 Getty Images
177 Getty Images
178 Getty Images
180 (1) AFP/Getty Images
180 (2) Getty Images
180 (3) AFP/Getty Images
180 (4) Getty Images
182 Getty Images
183 Getty Images
183 Getty Images
183 Getty Images
183 Getty Images
183 Getty Images
184 Getty Images
185 Getty Images
185 Getty Images
186 Getty Images
186 Getty Images
186 Getty Images
187 Getty Images
188 (t) © Crown Copyright/MOD 2012
188 (b) Getty Images
189 Getty Images

When images are not numbered:
(l) left, (r) right, (b) bottom, (t) top